ILEX FOUNDATION SERIES 28

MOBILITY AND MASKS

Also in the Ilex Foundation Series

more at www.ilexfoundation.org

MOBILITY AND MASKS: CULTURAL IDENTITY IN TRAVEL LITERATURE

edited by
Elizabeth C. Goldsmith

Ilex Foundation
Boston, Massachusetts

Distributed by Harvard University Press
Cambridge, Massachusetts and London, England

Mobility and Masks: Cultural Identity in Travel Literature
edited by Elizabeth C. Goldsmith

Published by Ilex Foundation, Boston, Massachusetts

Distributed by Harvard University Press, Cambridge, Massachusetts and London, England

Production editor: Christopher Dadian
Cover design: Joni Godlove
Printed in the United States of America

Cover image: *Abstract Head: Symphony in Pink* (1929). Oil on canvas, mounted on cardboard, by Alexej von Jawlensky. Städel Museum, Frankfurt am Main.

Library of Congress Cataloging-in-Publication Data

Names: Goldsmith, Elizabeth C., editor.
Title: Mobility and masks : cultural identity in travel literature / edited
   by Elizabeth C. Goldsmith.
Description: Boston, Massachusetts : Ilex Foundation ; Cambridge,
   Massachusetts : Distributed by Harvard University Press, [2024] |
   Series: Ilex Foundation series ; 28 | "The essays in this collection
   grew out of conversations among members of the Boston University Faculty
   Research Group for Travel Literature, culminating in a symposium on
   "Travel, Masks, Disguise" held in May 2022"--Introduction. | Includes
   bibliographical references. | Summary: "Travelers have always
   experimented with disguise while observing the disguises of others. Each
   of the chapters in Mobility and Masks illustrates the strategies of
   concealment in the experience of travel"-- Provided by publisher.
Identifiers: LCCN 2023057502 | ISBN 9780674295803 (paperback)
Subjects: LCSH: Travel in literature. | Travelers' writings--History and
   criticism. | Masks in literature. | Disguise in literature. |
   Travelers--Psychology. | Travel--Psychological aspects. | Travel--Social
   aspects. | Group identity. | LCGFT: Essays. | Literary criticism.
Classification: LCC PN56.T7 M63 2024 | DDC 809/.9332--dc23/eng/20240125
LC record available at https://lccn.loc.gov/2023057502

Contents

Foreword

IS IT POSSIBLE TO LIVE WITHOUT MASKS? Moralists, visionaries, and the politi-
cally pure have tried to make the case. In the Renaissance, illustrators fash-
ioned images of *Sincerity* as nude figures whose hearts are on display through
an open window on their chest. Some are trampling crumpled masks. Michel
de Montaigne, who embraced the identity of an "*honnête homme*," called those
whose affairs were hidden beneath a mask cowardly and servile. Reacting against
the legacy of Louis XIV's Versailles and its polished insincerity, eighteenth-
century writers denounced an entire society's pervasive falseness. Jean-Jacques
Rousseau, who called the man of the world "complete in his mask," was among
the most eloquent of his generation to call for unmasking. Each instance was a
response to the harm to humanity these writers believed masking brought. They
denounced the masks at court, among society's elites, in public places, and in
private conversation. They were minority voices. Most have learned to live with
masks.

As in many domains, Friedrich Nietzsche was a prophet of the present
concerning masks. In *Beyond Good and Evil*, he wrote that every profound spirit
loves a mask. The particular depths he had in mind – the realization that hardness, force, cruelty, and exploitation serve to enhance humanity – has its own
ancient affinities with masks. The roots of the word *mask* are from pre-Indo-
European sources in Italy's Piedmontese and Ligurian dialects to designate
witches. In ancient texts, *masca* often appeared with the Latin *striga*, a creature
from the underworld who poisoned children. The demonic and unearthly
associations of masks run from Dionysus to Harlequin, the latter a commedia
dell'arte character whose earliest embodiment was Herlaking, a mythical ruler
possessed by Satan who raced through the countryside on a ghostly steed.

Nietzsche's "profound spirit" points as well to the modern world, in which
the mask is a central figure for the psyche. He lived at a time when Freud and
others were discovering the uncharted realm of the unconscious. Freud's psycho-
analytic project was a kind of unmasking, and the reality it revealed was every
bit as troubling as the creatures who poisoned children and were possessed by
demons. In the Fin de Siècle, the Belgian painter James Ensor filled canvases
with anguished, mask-like faces. The French decadent artist Félicien Rops
painted syphilitic prostitutes whose masks smile sweetly. Modern masks hide
more than our physical features.

The uses of masks are multiple and contradictory. Masks of course conceal identities, but they may also reveal truths. Oscar Wilde captured a recognizable experience in "The Critic as Artist" when he declared that man is least himself when he speaks in his own person. "Give him a mask," he wrote, "and he will tell you the truth."[1] The insight was already known in the nineteenth century. "Men write better in a mask than for themselves," Emerson confided in his journal in 1841. An ancient fable, "Of the Hidden Face," conveys the power of masks to bring truth to light in another sense. Ashamed of his own foulness, a man aspiring to purity dons the radiant mask of a young saint. His wisdom eventually draws a band of disciples. Nearing death, he removes his mask, which reveals a face of divine beauty. "Master," a disciple asks, "why have you worn a mask that is the exact likeness of your face?"[2]

Masks can mark subordination or inspire independence. They are by turns conservative, fixing social position in hierarchical societies, and riotously disruptive. When conditions are explosive, carnival's exuberance can turn to sudden violence and even revolution. Masks may also serve to support the social order. For more than a century, Venetians wore masks nine months of the year to bring smooth relations among social unequals. Masks were common in the markets, in the theater, in cafes and the city's gambling hall, and in diplomatic dinners and receptions. Genuine anonymity was not the aim. The mask, rather, allowed all to act as if identities were unknown, which exempted wearers from the expected rituals of deference and subordination in the most unequal of societies. In this sense, they were conservative. They protected rather than denied rank and worked to bridge the chasm of hierarchy without ever denying it.

Women in particular experienced the opportunities these practices provided. In the seventeenth century in both Italy and France, women covered their faces when they appeared in public. Many claimed that this was a sign of subordination: a protection of supposedly fragile virtue. The more common motive was to maintain a psychological distance where physical distance was lacking.[3] They granted women a degree of freedom otherwise absent. A character in one of Goldoni's plays praises the independence this brings: "masks permit women to go everywhere honestly."[4]

Such a context reveals the original sense of *incognito*, an Italian coinage,

1. Oscar Wilde, "The Critic as Artist," in *De Profundis, The Ballad of Reading Gaol, and Other Writings* (Ware, England: Wordsworth Classics, 1999), 225.

2. See David Le Breton, *Des Visages* (Paris: Editions Métailie, 2003), 216.

3. See James H. Johnson, *Venice Incognito: Masks in the Serene Republic* (Berkeley: University of California Press, 2011), 114–17.

4. Carlo Goldoni, *Le donne di buon umore*, in *Tutte le opere*, 14 vols. (Milan: A. Mondadori, 1935–56), 6:1025.

which described identities known but not acknowledged. A French author in the early 1700s recommended that members of the high nobility dress in clothes that conveyed their status and identity even when masked, lest they be mistaken. "When they wish to go incognito, it is prudent for a prince and great lords to mask themselves nobly in a way that will always distinguish them from those who are common, so as not to be exposed to incidents that might otherwise arise."[5] Our own version of incognito – wearing sunglasses on the train or bus – serves similar purposes. It asserts a distance without relying on disguise, gives license to ignore others (and be ignored), and, as sometimes happened in more stratified societies, bring an intimacy in conversation that might not occur without them.

The variety and ubiquity of masks suggest the near impossibility of living without them. From antiquity, their proximity not merely to human interaction but to human identity itself has been present. The Romans called Greek tragic and comic masks a *persōna* based on their design to amplify actors' voices (*personāre*, "to sound through"). Etymologically every person is a persona, someone who plays a role. In ancient Rome, to be a person also carried legal status, which was denied to women and slaves. Selfhood itself wears a mask.

This volume offers a broad view of masking, both physical and figurative, as seen through the common frame of travel. The connection is manifestly rich. To leave one's own home for foreign spaces urges adaptation: to observe, chronicle, communicate, learn from, defy, or reject. Each act requires a suspension of accustomed habits and vocabularies. A traveler's mask may be a genuine disguise and therefore conceal. It may be an incognito, signaling status and even revealing identity while erecting the right defenses to forestall its acknowledgment. Masks may reveal a truth – temperamental, psychological, sexual – previously unacknowledged by the traveler. Masks women assume while traveling may be freeing in ways inaccessible to locals and inconceivable at home. As in the fable of the hidden face, a travelers' masks may come to transform their face to such an extent that it becomes impossible to return home.

Mobility and Masks: Cultural Identity in Travel Literature ranges from the ancient world to twentieth-century China and Russia. The masks these essays identify and seek to penetrate are a sampling of the many sources and strategies of concealment. They treat personae and the psyche in authors who capture others' inner experience through the imagination. They find more modern embodiments of the ancient association of the underworld with masks. They describe travelers whose masks of dress or comportment are turned to challenge accustomed categories, challenging dominant views of race, religion, or beauty.

5. Jacques Bonnet, *Histoire générale de la danse* (Paris: Houry, 1724), 152.

There are repeated instance of women who find in the mask a means of independence. This collection of essays is an original and perceptive contribution to the continued presence of masks across human societies.

James H. Johnson

author of *Venice Incognito: Masks in the Serene Republic* (2011), and *Paris Concealed: Masks in the City of Light* (forthcoming from University of Chicago Press)

Acknowledgments

THIS BOOK RESULTS from the ongoing work of the Boston University Faculty Research Group on Travel Literature. We have enjoyed lively conversations in the challenging times of recent years, when masking has been obligatory and travel difficult. For support in organizing the workshop that enabled us to share early versions of the essays in this volume, thanks is due to the Department of World Languages and Literatures and the Department of Classical Studies at Boston University. I am especially grateful to Christopher Dadian of the Ilex Foundation for his careful editorial work.

Introduction

Elizabeth C. Goldsmith

IN THE EXPERIENCE OF THE TRAVELER, the concept and practice of masking seems always to be present, if extremely variable. Travel and disguise go together frequently, in the accounts written by modern adventurers as well as historical ones. Writing in the 1930s Robert Byron, in *The Road to Oxiana*, disguises himself in order to break through bureaucratic barriers that prevent him from seeing and photographing the Persian monuments that so fascinate him. There are contemporary travelers like Paul Theroux for whom travel perpetually involves some kind of performance. In his book *The Great Railway Bazaar* he always seems to view himself as playing a role, on stage and masked, supremely reluctant to reveal anything about himself on his travels while wanting constantly to unmask others. There are travelers like Isabelle Eberhardt who in the 1890s dressed as a man as she traveled through Algeria, to protect herself but also to embrace risk and somehow try to become a suffering version of the people she met on her wanderings.

The traveler prizes what is new and destabilizing, welcoming the promise of knowledge that will come from an encounter with unfamiliar cultures. And yet travelers often associate the success of their voyage not only with their skill at penetrating the veils that always seem to disguise encounters on their travels, they also seek to better understand precisely that which has always been familiar to them, when they eventually return home. The experience of travel adds to the force of that recognition, so that, like Ulysses, when travelers return they have gained an understanding and an appreciation of what they had known before, by a process of re-cognition that they never could have attained without embarking on a voyage. It has become a familiar trope of travel narrative that the return home involves a kind of unmasking, enabling the traveler to achieve a deeper knowledge of the familiar.

To travel, to learn from experience often seems to involve a heightened consciousness of masking on the part of the traveler, an awareness of how all encounters with the new or the foreign necessarily involve hiding oneself or observing how others do the same. In what is probably the best-known travel narrative in world literature, *The Odyssey*, the heroic traveler is successful in surviving his voyage and ultimately returning home largely because of his cunning and his skill at using disguises. Ulysses is never far from an adventure in masking, either

1

disguising himself or cleverly seeing through the veils put on by others. And the end of his voyage when he finally returns home is a moment of masking followed by recognition, as his old nurse sees through his disguise and recognizes him for who he truly is.

Travel invites a crossing of the boundaries of identity as well as space. This is never more apparent than in the European accounts of early encounters with the "New World," whether written by explorers, adventurers, scientists, missionaries, or colonialists. Certain periods and places seem to promote a heightened cultural awareness of masking and disguise. This is true of court societies such as that of early modern France, which produced writers and thinkers for whom strategic deception was a fundamental way of being. "The world is composed only of appearances," wrote La Rochefoucauld.[1] Pascal probed this worldview further, and declared that humans universally disguise themselves not only to others, but to themselves. For Pascal, the desire to travel, or even to leave the solitude of one's room, is enough to set one on the path of perpetual deception, self-deception, and misery.[2]

For others, viewing life as a perpetual masquerade could be a source of both pleasure and wisdom. In Venice, ritual masking was at the heart of cultural life, reaching its apex in the eighteenth century, by which time all of Venetian society donned masks for nine months out of the year. This was not simply an extension of Carnival season, it had more to do with theater. And like theater actors, Venetians did not wear masks to disguise themselves but rather to enable a kind of fluidity of identity. As James Johnson writes, the purpose of masking was more about "preserving distance, guarding status, and permitting contact among unequals through fictive concealment."[3]

While Venice may have perfected the art of masking and its liberating effects, enabling a mixing of social identifiers of all kinds: class, gender, religion, income, profession, ethnicity, national identity, and race, other societies in the pre-modern period experimented freely with the practice of masquerade. Certain kinds of masking became closely associated with the experience of travel. Travelers who returned home with tales and illustrations of their encounters with foreign peoples inspired their audiences to reproduce their accounts in costume, portraits, and masks. A range of court spectacles routinely saw aristocrats dressed up in the costumes of people who had been described by travelers, who sometimes returned

1. La Rochefoucauld 2007, 73.

2. "We are nothing but lies, duplicity, contradiction, and we hide and disguise ourselves from ourselves." Pascal 1999, 127.

"I have often said that man's unhappiness springs from one thing alone, his incapacity to stay quietly in one room." Pascal 1999, 44.

3. Johnson 2011, xii.

from their voyages accompanied by "examples" of the exotic people they had encountered: Indians, Africans, Brazilians, Turks.[4] This type of spectacle soon extended to a broader public in the form of popular masquerade balls. Fashionable costumes worn at masked balls were often inspired by illustrations of indigenous men and women published in travel accounts.[5]

In the many accounts written by travelers to Venice who observe the psychological effects of masking and masquerade, and in French commentary on costume and fashion as it evolved from the practices of masquerade, there is a repeated insistence on the liberating effects of masking and costuming. The wearer of a mask, disguise, or foreign costume will feel able to discover new identities in themselves, and as they view others, they will see new types of "truths" unveiled. This is analogous to the experience of the early traveler who, having learned to veil their own identity to enhance their acceptance in foreign lands, claims to have learned to unveil and recognize the "natural" beauty of exotic peoples.[6]

Some travelers focus repeatedly on descriptions of this experience in their accounts and letters home. They emphasize how they have learned to move freely and unnoticed in foreign cultures. Their descriptions can be competitive – every traveler wants to claim that they have a superior understanding of the culture they are describing, compared to authors of other travel accounts. An important marker of this superiority is the ability to unveil what is hidden to the untrained eye, to see behind what is masked or normally uncomprehended. The seventeenth-century French traveler to Mughal India, Francois Bernier, emphasizes in his travel accounts the importance of having different personas that he could assume, depending on the type of access he required. He was able to function as doctor, philosopher, translator, educator, or spiritual advisor, using these fluid identities to cultivate different contacts. For him, this ability to shift identities in a foreign culture was also liberating compared to his life in France, where his social and personal status was much more firmly prescribed.[7]

Early female travelers were eager to experiment with ways in which their gender gave them special access to social scenarios from which men were excluded, enabling them to comprehend aspects of the culture that men could not. In Mary Wortley Montagu's descriptions of her visits to Turkish baths for women, she exposes the false claims of previous accounts written by men, focusing in-

4. On this see Riello 2019 and Roux 2019. Pan-European interest in and emulation of Ottoman culture was particularly strong, as evidenced in masquerade as well as fashion, diplomacy, and trade. See Landweber 2005 and Bevilaqua and Pfeifer 2013.

5. Cohen 1999, 186.

6. Cohen 1999, 186.

7. On Bernier's reflections on his own identity and how his extensive travels transformed it, see Tinguely 2008.

stead on her own ability to take a realistic view of the scenes that for men could only amount to a fantasy.[8] In her account, this conventionally imagined space of female confinement is in fact a site of public sociability comparable to the male dominated English coffeehouse. And she describes how the Turkish women looked askance at her own inhibiting costume, a dress with corset and stays, and concluded that it must have been required of her by a controlling husband.[9]

The essays in this collection explore the multifaceted ways in which disguise, identity shifting, and masking are represented as central to the experience of the traveler in world literature from antiquity to the present day. Our volume explores the elements of masks, *persona*, and disguise in travel narratives across time. The wide range of times and places discussed, and the inclusion of both fictional and nonfictional accounts are intentional. We are interested in exploring the responses recorded by travelers to encounters with experiences and cultures that were new and distant to themselves and to their readers. The knowledge that they do draw on is frequently taken from fiction, just as fictional travel stories often are inspired by real travel narratives.

The opening chapter, by **James Uden,** examines some poems written by Horace that contemplate the implications of mobility, either freely indulged or ruthlessly denied. While travel was an experience common to almost everyone in Roman antiquity, much of it was forced mobility, whether through kidnapping, slavery, war, or exile. Uden studies the different veiled identities that Horace uses, focusing on the voice of his enslaved *vilicus* or overseer, and the voice of a runaway slave. Poetic voice here is used as mask, one that facilitates a fantasy of escape, travel, and mobility. This poetic "ventriloquism" leads Horace to achieve a measure of "slave subjectivity" that others have not recognized in readings of these poems. In Horace's description of his journeys, he invokes fantasies of travel that lead him to enjoy an imagined world completely independent from external constraints. His intimate connections to slavery as both an owner of slaves and the son of a freedman are woven into these poems as he uses masking as a vehicle of imagination and invokes mobility as a register of social power.

Sunil Sharma's chapter explores the figure of the "masked" or disguised woman as a classic obstacle to the heroic traveler, drawing on examples from Ariosto's Renaissance epic poem *Orlando Furioso* and the collection of Middle Eastern folktales known as *One Thousand and One Nights*. In these and many other accounts of travel and adventure, men who encounter beautiful women on their travels are often trapped by them. In the two works considered here, the women frequently turn out to be witches or angry hags. Sharma looks closely at the "crafty crones" themselves and the ways in which they are depicted as conscious-

8. Montagu 1835, Letter 29.
9. On this description, see Spencer 2016.

ly exploiting their masks. Some of the most striking characters of this type in both Western and Oriental literature are associated with travel: they take on their crafty disguises when they embark on a voyage with an eye to avenge themselves or interfere with the progress of the hero's quest. As women, moreover, they must disguise themselves in order to be successful travelers. Phobia about the traveling woman takes its most extreme form in the image of the witch, whose mobility is supernatural, allowing them to fly anywhere. The successful traveler is associated with toughness and hardness, which in a woman is seen to betray her nature.

Elizabeth C. Goldsmith studies the travels of Sophia of Hanover as described in her memoirs and letters written in the late seventeenth century. She follows Sophia's gradual recognition of the range of uses that she can make of the practice of traveling incognito, then a routinely accepted way for elite voyagers to ease the burden of protocol and ceremony when traveling to foreign courts. Masking, in Sophia's experience, is an inevitable part of living as a public figure, but Sophia seems to be looking for a way of living comfortably with a mask. For her, to exist utterly without seeking to hide oneself to some degree is out of the question, even inconceivable. And unmasking, recognizing the strategies used by others to disguise themselves, is an important objective in Sophia's travels, as a way of confirming her skill at accessing "truth." She takes the measure of her own growing sophistication at this as she travels, and as she comes to understand how the game of masking is crucial to being able to successfully negotiate the world.

Sophia of Hanover's reflections on incognito travel, and her experiments with it, lead her to develop a measure of personal independence, and eventually a kind of freedom to discover and express her own character. Traveling incognito can be in her mind a virtue, and almost a way of living that gives her a deeper sense of freedom than simply a freedom from the material trappings of her rank. Her memoir, inspired by an episode of tension in her marriage and thoughts of her own mortality, records her discoveries, on the road, of the ever-present importance of the mask.

Eugenio Menegon's chapter on "the habit of the monk" explores how clothing and fashion became important aspects of Italian Jesuit missionary strategies in seventeenth- and eighteenth-century China. The missionaries observed, sometimes to their own dismay, that they would have to abandon the practice of wearing the clerical habit and costume themselves in silk garments appropriate for courtiers or literati if they wanted to earn the respect of those they were trying to convert. The traditional habit of the monk was closely tied to their Christian identity, so that abandoning these pious, simple garments in favor of richer clothing felt to many missionaries like a mask, a pretentious falsifying of their identity. At the same time, it was argued that "blending in" and taking on clothing styles, beards, and hats that would encourage people to view the Jesuits as authoritative and wise, would help further their missionary purpose. For the Jesuit travelers, it became essential to learn how to hide their religious identity at least temporarily, in order to facilitate their engagement with the local population.

The missionary community developed rationales for their new wardrobes, as both necessary to life in a new climate and useful in their religious mission. They developed their own rules and restraints on the extravagance of their new attire in response to the concern that the practice of disguise would become a source of pleasure more than a necessary strategy serving religious conversion.

In her chapter on eighteenth-century metropolitan travelers writing about the West Indies, **Manuela Coppola** examines accounts that describe creole women as wearing white "masks." Focusing on the journal and letters of Janet Schaw, who traveled to Antigua, St. Kitts, and North Carolina in the 1770s, Coppola traces how creoles were accorded a precarious identity in contemporary descriptions that drew on images of tainted women who were unsuccessful in their efforts to mimic white Englishness. Schaw's travel narrative addresses the "otherness" of creoles and marginalized white inhabitants of the English colonies. She struggles to explain their difference, but in so doing also reflects on racial identity as a performance, holding up a mirror to herself and other European travelers. The portraits of others that Schaw composes in her writing can also be read as multiple reflections of herself. Coppola includes a discussion of paintings that were made to be reproduced in travel accounts of the West Indies, and were published in an effort to attract more Europeans to the colonies. She emphasizes the masking functions of these illustrations, how they played into a view of West Indian society as a "perpetual masquerade party" where distinctions of status were blurred or distorted.

Mary Beth Raycraft writes about one of the few nineteenth-century French women to travel to Asia and publish their account of the experience. Laure Durand-Fardel traveled with her physician husband to Shanghai in 1875. Her letters describe how she experimented with different personas on her voyage, exploring her new life as traveler, writer, and collector of objects from Asian material culture. She pushed herself to develop original perspectives on Asian culture that would enlighten her readers in an age when images of China and Japan were being circulated to a curious and interested public at home. Durand-Fardel's observations as a woman traveler often seem to relate to a kind of unmasking project, either "demystifying" her reader's preconceptions or more literally casting an objective eye on practices like footbinding, in her long description of watching a Chinese woman's feet being unwrapped. She gives particular attention to foreign notions of female beauty that involve distortion, both cosmetic (teeth blackening) and physical (footbinding), and emphasizes her own privileged position as a traveling woman who is able to reveal how these masking practices are implemented. Like

Mary Wortley Montagu, and other women travel writers studied in this volume, Durand-Fardel claims her own special ability to lift the veils that other travelers cannot penetrate. She enjoys unmasking the claims of women's beauty that male-authored travel accounts routinely inserted in their descriptions of place.

Roberta Micallef's essay studies the concept of masking and "passing" as deployed in the story of an Arab immigrant to Holland by the contemporary Finland-based Iraqi author Hasan Blasim. The character Salim Abdul Hussain changes his name and his outer demeanor, struggling to discard his native language and learn a difficult new one, all in order to more successfully transform himself into a true citizen of his adopted homeland. He tries to internalize cultural attitudes in his environment, including hostility toward his native Arab culture. But rather than becoming Dutch, he becomes increasingly aware of himself as playing a role. Masking, in this classic scenario of the modern immigrant, is an existential effort with a lofty goal of self-transformation. Unlike the masking strategies used by travelers who wish to better negotiate, temporarily, a foreign landscape, the efforts of the immigrant refugee are impossible to realize, if only because they require a complete erasure of one's past self. Micallef's essay explores the trope of the traveler as identity-shifter, pointing to the ways in which, unlike a figure from a classic travel narrative, the main character of Blasim's story is unable to learn from his masking. He is a traveler who can never return to his origins to enjoy the recognition and enhanced familiarity of home.

Catherine Yeh's chapter examines the process of cultural transmission as it was enacted in a historic visit of the famous Chinese actor Mei Lanfang to Russia in 1935. This was an important moment in relations between China and Russia as well as with European artists sympathetic to the Soviet artistic agenda. Yeh looks at how Mei Lanfang's dramatic techniques were interpreted, transmitted, and translated into Western terms in order to be better understood by Russian and European audiences. The inevitable masking and "cultural camouflage" that this process required is, she argues, to some degree always present in transcultural encounters. For meaningful cultural migration to take place, there is always some misdirection, some veiling that amounts to a kind of translation of one conceptual framework into another, a "localization" process that facilitates understanding. In the case of Mei Lanfang, he understood that his planned expositions from Chinese opera would have to undergo this kind of translation. Yeh looks specifically at the demands of socialist realism, which had been officially codified one year prior to Mei Lanfang's visit, to see how the Chinese artist came to understand what masks and distortions he would have to accept in the transmission of his art in order to give it a place in the new Soviet aesthetic agenda. Moreover, Mei Lanfang came to understand how the Western (mis)interpretations of Chinese opera, particularly the embrace of Chinese opera as modern, symbolic art with roots in folk culture, could help protect the traditional form from attacks at home, and challenges to its relevancy for modern society and politics.

The essays in this collection grew out of conversations among members of the Boston University Faculty Research Group for Travel Literature, culminating in a symposium on "Travel, Masks, Disguise" held in May 2022. As we explored the topic of masking and travel, we came to understand the experience of the disguised traveler, and the traveler observing disguises, as fundamental to the process of cultural transmission, the development of cultural identity, and their representations. This is true of real travel accounts as well as fictional ones that describe the shock of contact with the unknown. Our collection ends, then, with an essay that addresses a question threading through all of these very diverse looks at the process and practice of masking in the traveler's experience. Masking inevitably mediates the encounter of strangers, just as it does all early contacts of one culture with another. As an artist, Mei Lanfang understood the impossibility of unmediated cultural transmission and in the process he reflected on how the "foreign" gaze could impact his art, and lead to ways of renewing and refreshing traditional art forms when he returned home.

BIBLIOGRAPHY

Bernier, François. 1699. *Voyages de François Bernier*. Amsterdam.

Bevilaqua, Alexander and Helen Pfeifer. 2013. "Turquerie: Culture in Motion." *Past and Present*, no. 221 (November): 75–118.

Byron, Robert. 1937. *The Road to Oxiana*. London.

Cohen, Sarah. 1999. "Masquerade as Mode in the French Fashion Print." In *The Clothes That Wear Us: Essays on Dressing and Transgressing in Eighteenth-Century Culture*, edited by Jessica Munns and Penny Richards, 174–208. Newark, NJ.

Eberhardt, Isabelle. 1906. *Dans l'ombre chaude de l'Islam*. Paris.

Johnson, James. 2011. *Venice Incognito: Masks in the Serene Republic*. Berkeley.

Landweber, Julia. 2005. "Celebrating Identity: Charting the History of Turkish Masquerade in Early Modern France." *Romance Studies* 23 (3): 175–89.

La Rochefoucauld, François, duc de. 2007. *Collected Maxims and Other Reflections*. Oxford, UK.

Montagu, Mary Wortley. 1835. *Letters of Lady M. W. Montagu during the Embassy to Constantinople, 1716–18*. London.

Pascal, Blaise. 1999. *Pensées and Other Writings*. Oxford, UK.

Riello, Giorgio. 2019. "The World in a Book: The Creation of the Global in Sixteenth-Century European Costume Books." *Past and Present*, Supplement 14: 281–317.

Roux, Benoît. 2019. "Entrer dans la danse: *Les Sauvages* de Rameau." In *Kalína-go, Histoire(s) caraïbe(s) – XVIᵉ-XVIIᵉ siècles*, 2019–12–07. https://kalinago. hypotheses.org/951.

Theroux, Paul. 1975. *The Great Railway Bazaar: By Train through Asia*. Boston.

Tinguely, Frédéric. 2008. "Introduction." In *Un libertin dans l'Inde Moghole: Les voyages de François Bernier (1656–1669)*, edited by F Tinguely, 7–34. Paris.

Spencer, Vicki A. 2016. "Lady Mary Wortley Montagu and the Women's Coffee House." In *Feminist Moments: Reading Feminist Texts*, edited by Katherine Smits and Susan Bruce, 35–42. London.

Chapter 1

Freedom to Travel: Slavery and Mobility in Horace

James Uden

FOR THE ROMAN POET HORACE, yearning to travel was a sign of the unquiet mind. Only those not sufficiently in control of their own souls have the desire to flit from place to place, never content in any one location and endlessly seeking something new. In *Epistles* 1.11, published c. 20–19 BCE, he addresses an otherwise unknown friend named "Bullatius," who has been traveling around the eastern part of the Empire. Bullatius' name recalls the *bulla*, the amulet worn around the neck of Roman children to signify their free status, and indeed freedom is one of Horace's key concerns in the poem. "We seek the good life on ships and chariots," says Horace, yet in fact "energetic idleness exhausts us all" (strenua nos exercet inertia; navibus atque / quadrigis petimus bene vivere, *Epistles* 1.11.28–29). Happiness can be found anywhere the soul is at ease. The vanity of travel is encapsulated in one of Horace's most memorable and excerptible tags, endlessly revoiced by future generations of travelers and travel writers: "those who hasten across the ocean change their clime, not their mind" (caelum, non animum, mutant qui trans mare currunt, *Epistles* 1.11.27). Horace's advice to Bullatius is clear. Be grateful for whatever you have. Seize opportunities when they come. Do not, however, seek liberation from your troubles in travel, because only wisdom and reason can take away your cares.

Travel was a constant part of ancient experience, especially in a major, multicultural metropolis like Rome, where nearly everyone had arrived from somewhere else. Much of that movement, however was *forced* mobility, since a large proportion of the enslaved population at Rome – as much as a quarter of the total population – would have been trafficked from elsewhere through trade, kidnapping, piracy, and war.[1] It has long been a standard lament of classicists that we have no first-person accounts of that experience, but that view has been importantly revised by Amy Richlin's monumental *Slave Theater in the Roman Republic: Plautus and Popular Comedy* (2017). Taking seriously an ancient tradi-

---

1. Quantifying the enslaved population at Rome is notoriously difficult. Scheidel 2011 examines the late Republic to early Empire (first century BCE – first century CE) and estimates that 15–25% of the total population was enslaved. Slavery in ancient Rome was a civic and legal status, not based on race. It was frequently temporary, though the ease of manumission in the ancient world should not be overstated. For Horace on travel, see Skalitzky 1973.

tion that the Roman playwright Plautus was enslaved for some part of his life, questioning the standard idea that his surviving plays were composed and per-formed for "elites," and treating the protests and laments of Plautus' comic slave characters as fragments of subjective experience rather than stylized variations on literary tropes, Richlin effectively uncovers an entire archive of ancient testimony about the life and emotions of the enslaved.[2] Free and forced movement loom large as themes in those comedies. As Richlin writes, the "scenarios of slavery and enslavement require insistent questions: what is your *patria*? Where are you from? What was your name? Who were your parents?"[3] Characters in comic plots criss-cross the ancient Mediterranean either on military expeditions and business trips (if they are free), or as victims of human trafficking and imagined escapes (if they are enslaved). In Rome as in later cultures, social status was closely associated with physical mobility, and travel represented a valuable form of social currency. "No characteristic of slaves' statelessness," writes Linda K. Kerber, has been "more obvious than their lack of freedom to travel."[4]

The actors in Plautus' comedies were almost certainly wearing masks, al-though the interplay of identities between mask and actor must have been com-plex. In many cases enslaved actors would have been playing the theatrical role of the 'slave', and so their words were constantly charged with a meaningful ambiguity about whose reality they were speaking, whose part they were play-ing.[5] Horace, writing almost two centuries later, did not write comedies, but he too puts on the mask of the slave periodically in his poems, most memorably in *Satires* 2.7, a dialogue in which Horace imagines the enslaved Davus using the temporary freedom of the Saturnalia festival to remind Horace of his faults. In his

2. Richlin 2017, 21. Recent work has followed similar paths: Culik-Baird 2019 emphasizes the ways in which performances of Roman tragedy may have dramatized the experience of being captured in war, and Keith 2021 has explored the realities of human trafficking and sex slavery that underlie the romantic fictions of the Roman love elegists. This work is a significant departure from the earlier approach epitomized by studies such as Fitzgerald 2000, which took their cue from the ubiquitous metaphorization of the master-slave relationship in antiquity, and viewed slavery in Latin literature largely as a means through which free authors envisaged aspects of themselves. Fitzgerald began his study by effectively abandoning any hope of recovering the perspective of enslaved people: "slavery was too much an unquestioned part of the way things were for the experience of the slave to be conceived as an object of interest" (at page 2).

3. Richlin 2017, 351. Richlin lists the travel destinations mentioned in the extant plays at pages 352–54. See also Isayev 2017, 191–228; Duffalo 2021, 27–61.

4. Kerber 2005, 733, cited by Pryor 2016, 104. On slave mobility in the ancient world, see especially Joshel 2013, who details the strategies employed on Roman agricultural estates to curtail and surveil the movement of enslaved people. Cf. Pryor 2016, 46 on nineteenth-century America: the "notion that African Americans who traveled on their own were doing so unlawfully and were thus dangerous created an attendant system of surveillance that deputized all white Americans – slaveholders and non-slaveholders alike – to interrogate, harass, arrest, seize, and discipline people of color who dared to move outside of those spaces designated for black use by whites."

5. For what we know about masks in Plautus, see Marshall 2006, 136–40.

case, too, there was a complex interplay between mask and actor. Horace's own father had been enslaved and manumitted, in circumstances that are now (perhaps deliberately) irrecoverable to readers of his verse. Horace's contemporaries remembered that indignity, or so he tells us. In a series of texts Horace defiantly reclaims the mantle of "son of a freedman father," either to praise the ingenuousness of men like Maecenas who welcomed him into their fold for his talent rather than his wealth or nobility (*Satires* 1.6.45–64), or to accentuate his own achievement in having risen to such heights from such slim beginnings (*Epistles* 1.20.19–22). He owes his entire moral education to his father, he boasts, who taught him to live frugally and to avoid the extravagant vices that ruin others (*Satires* 1.4.105–29). This description has seemed to many readers a little too close to stereotypical scenes in ancient comedy of strict fathers reproving wayward sons, and has accordingly been read as the poet's translation of his own autobiography into literary tropes.[6] But a truth stylized may still be a truth. Wouldn't they have talked? If Horace's father had spoken to his son about the trauma of slavery – if he had taught his son how to get by on little, for example, having known a time when nothing he had was his own – then the insistent theme of slavery in Horace's own work may well preserve fragments of his father's experience. Given readers' awareness of slavery in Horace's family history, the mask of the slave in Horace's texts cannot simply be read as an elite appropriation of enslaved experience, or as the direct expression of "slave subjectivity." It must have wavered uncertainly between the two.[7]

This essay focuses on two poems of Horace that center upon mobility and travel, but which stand outside the usual set of texts considered travel poems in Horace's oeuvre (*Epistles* 1.11; *Satires* 1.5; *Odes* 1.3). In *Epistles* 1.14, Horace addresses the enslaved farm manager (*vilicus*) on his agricultural estate, contrasting the manager's discontented desire to travel to the city with his own longing to stay on the estate. Horace is, of course, free to move. His *vilicus'* dreams of travel, by contrast, are much more likely dreams of escape, and his mobility is scripted and curtailed by his free slaveowner. *Odes* 1.22 offers a more fantastical vision of travel. The poet imagines a miraculous occurrence on his estate in which he escaped a dangerous encounter with a wolf, and that anecdote is set within a series of descriptions of imagined journeys to far-flung places in the Empire. Here the shadow of slavery is less easy to discern. But here too, I will argue, the freedom

---

6. Leach 1973; Muecke 1979, 67–68.

7. The phrase "slave subjectivity" is from Culik-Baird 2019, 177. Williams 1995 conjectured influentially that Horace's father was an influential citizen captured in Venusia and sold into slavery during the Social Wars of 89 BCE, and that pretensions of low birth are deliberately crafted to suit Horace's self-image. Horace's silence on all this seems important. He deliberately extracts slavery from the particulars of his father's case, and yet it remains plausible that the trauma of his father's enslavement shaped his own vision of Roman social relationships.

of the interlocutor to roam securely around the world is contrasted implicitly with the poem's two other characters: the addressee Aristius Fuscus, who was potentially, like Horace's father, a freedman; and his beloved Lalage, who is of unspoken social status in the poem, but bears a name which is almost universally attested for enslaved women. Horace himself may be skeptical of the ethical value of travel. But that does not lessen its cachet for the free, for whom the privilege of mobility was intertwined with the restrictions on the movement of the enslaved.

MODES OF MOBILITY IN *EPISTLES* 1.14

Horace's *Epistles* 1.14 begins with a challenge. The *vilicus* hates the farm at which he has been stationed, and the poet invites us to see whether he can root out an ethical issue with greater zeal than the manager pulls out weeds at the farm (*Epistles* 1.14.1–5):

> Vilice silvarum et mihi me reddentis agelli,
> quem tu fastidis, habitatum quinque focis et
> quinque bonos solitum Variam dimittere patres,
> certemus, spinas animone ego fortius an tu
> evellas agro, et melior sit Horatius an res.[8]

> *Vilicus* of my woods and of the humble farm that returns me to myself –
> the farm you loathe, though it offers home and hearth to five,
> and regularly sends five worthy men on to the town of Varia –
> let us compete. Can I pull the thorns from my own mind with more
>   strength
> than you pull them from my land? Is Horace or his estate in better shape?

Critics have held widely varying opinions of Horace's treatment of the *vilicus*. "Horace, no doubt, genuinely cares for the slave and tries to prevent him from taking a false step," wrote Fraenkel.[9] Mayer praises Horace for being able to "put himself mentally into the slave's position," an attitude "remarkable in a free-born Roman," and "exemplary for his readers."[10] McGann is more circumspect: Horace begins on a note of gentle recrimination, but that tone grows icy at the poem's end, when the poet likens the *vilicus* to a pack-horse (*caballus*, 43), and the demotion of his addressee from sparring partner to work animal is a "final

---

8. The Latin text quoted is that of Shackleton Bailey 2008. Translations are my own.

9. Fraenkel 1957, 313. On the social status of the *vilicus*, Carlsen 1995, 57–70.

10. Mayer 1994, 213. Similarly generous is Kilpatrick 1986, 89, who claims that Horace reasons with the *vilicus* from an "intimate and affectionate understanding of his character," and Hiltbrunner 1974, 300, who describes the opening conflict of values as a "very friendly" (*sehr freundschaftliches*) dispute, and a way to welcome him into "humane" (*menschliche*) society.

assertion of Horace's will."[11] By contrast, Highet sees hardheartedness throughout *Epistles* 1.14, and indeed throughout Horace's descriptions of slaveholding. It is natural, says Highet, that Horace "wrote a good deal about slaves and slavery: the subject haunted him. But it is surprising to observe that his tone is seldom sympathetic, and often downright cruel."[12] Most extreme is Johnson, who bluntly asserts that Horace "feared and hated slaves" because of a lingering guilt and fear that he was very nearly one himself. Only his father's manumission separated him from the people he now owned, and that precarious closeness bred a deep hostility in the "buried places of his psyche."[13] It would be easy to dismiss such overt psychologizing as impressionistic, and yet Highet and Johnson pinpoint a streak of hostility and aggression that gentler readings of Horace mollify or ignore.

In fact, simmering hostility is evident from the opening lines of *Epistles* 1.14. "Let us compete," says Horace (*certemus*, 4). The contest is uneven, and the slaveowner wins by default. More than a neat turn of phrase, the equivalence that the poet draws between rooting thorny problems from the mind and removing actual thorns from the ground sets the basic pattern for the poem. *Epistles* 1.14, and indeed the entire master-slave relationship, is based on false analogy. One will do mental work, and the other physical work, but the two are not and cannot be the same. Lines 1–5 of the poem also briefly sketch a hierarchy of power that is grounded in freedom of movement. First, when Horace says that his little plot "returns him to himself," he reminds the reader of the luxury of traveling to fulfill some spiritual need. Second is the tenant farmers, described in lines 2–3; they live on the property (*habitatum*, 2), but when they travel to the nearby town of Varia they too exhibit a freedom of movement that is impossible for the enslaved manager.[14] Third is the *vilicus*. As Horace reminds us, he is stuck in a place that he loathes. Or is it Horace he loathes? "Quem tu fastidis" (2): the relative pronoun refers grammatically to the closest masculine noun (*agelli*), but it is hard not to hear another direct object for that verb, since "mihi me" is repeated so emphatically before it.

The poem also begins with the claim that the farm makes Horace feel complete, and returns him to himself. The language is striking: it is as though some part of himself, some "fugitive subjectivity," has escaped his rational control and

11. McGann 1969, 69–70. Also mixed is Bowditch 2001, for whom the "egalitarian tone of friendly dialogue" at the start of *Epistles* 1.14 becomes at the end the "didactic command of a superior to an inferior" (at p. 238).

12. Highet 1973, 269.

13. Johnson 1993, 37; also at 44, 115. Yet Johnson says almost nothing about *Epistles* 1.14; it is odd that a book about the "dialectic of freedom" in *Epistles* 1 barely mentions the one poem addressed to someone who is enslaved.

14. Do they travel to sell their produce, or to perform some official function in the town (modern Vicovaro, northeast of Rome)? Lyne 1995, 6–7, opts for the latter.

needs to be returned.[15] One of the masks that Horace dons throughout his book of poetic *Epistles* is that of the *fugitivus* (runaway slave), and the ethics of his text are woven from constant imagery of bondage and escape. "I am like the *fugitivus*," he claims in *Epistles* 1.10, expressing a figurative desire to run away from the luxuries of the city.[16] In the very opening poem of the collection, he tells us that the mark of virtue is "fleeing from vice," and he compares himself to an old gladiator forced to fight again in the arena – "the metaphor suggests re-enslavement," comments Mayer.[17] Horace dons that mask of the *fugitivus* at various points throughout *Epistles* 1.14. The reason for discontent, he counsels, is in our mind, which "can never escape itself," a phrase that transforms ethical disquiet into a sort of spiritual slavery.[18] Similarly, when the poet tells the *vilicus* that he was delayed in Rome because he was caring for a friend, he said that he longed to "break the bonds (*claustra*) that blocked his course" (9) and return to his estate. Readers since antiquity have explained the image as an allusion to the racehorse ready to burst the bolts on the starting gates in a chariot race, but the image could equally recall the *fugitivus*; Pliny the Younger, in a later text, likened his friends' verses to runaways who have "broken their bonds" (*claustra sua refregerunt*), having slipped out to the public before publication.[19] When Horace says in the poem's first line, then, that his farm returns him to himself, he announces one of the poem's dominant metaphors. Some fugitive subjectivity has been righted and restored. An errant part of himself has been mastered.[20] The image is figurative for Horace, but not for the *vilicus,* who is unable to leave the farm he loathes. Perhaps there is a threat: if you escape, you too shall be returned.

At the center of the poem, Horace gives us his own vision of the sordid cityscape that the *vilicus* longs to visit (21–6):

> ... Fornix tibi et uncta popina
> incutiunt urbis desiderium, video, et quod
> angulus iste feret piper et tus ocius uua,
> nec vicina subest vinum praebere taberna

15. I take the term "fugitive subjectivity" from the analysis by Buzinde and Osagie 2011 of William Wells Brown's pioneering travel narrative *An American Fugitive in Europe* (1855).

16. *Epistles* 1.10.10–11; cf. *Satires* 2.7.113.

17. Mayer 1994, 87; *Epistles*. 1.1.19, 14, 41.

18. See McCarter 2015, 183, who notes this connection.

19. *Epistles* 2.10.3. Kenney 1977, 233–34 instead sees an allusion to the philosopher Epicurus in Lucretius' *De Rerum Natura* (1.70–1), who yearned to "break open the tight bonds of nature" with his mind.

20. The same verb (*reddere*) occurs in Horace, *Satires* 2.7.70–1 to describe the return of a slave to a master: "what beast, having broken his chains and escaped once, is so perverse as to return himself?" (quae belua ruptis / cum semel effugit, reddit se prava catenis?). Bowditch 2001 notes the thematic significance throughout Horace's oeuvre of the verb *reddere,* which frequently signifies the involvement of the "self in a system of exchanges" (at 232).

quae possit tibi nec meretrix tibicina, cuius   25
ad strepitum salias terrae grauis.

I see that the brothel and the greasy bar strike up
a desire for the city for you. This corner of countryside won't sprout
pepper and incense as quickly as it does grapes.
There's no tavern nearby that can offer you wine, nor
prostitutes to play their pipes, so you can stamp your
feet heavily on the floor to their sound.

The city that the *vilicus* longs to visit is painted in a series of broad stereotypes. All he *really* wants is sex, wine, pepper, and incense. Elite Romans ate and caroused in private dinner parties, which served as opportunities to reinforce ritualized social hierarchies. By contrast, Roman writers frequently depicted the tavern as unnervingly egalitarian, a space where the lower classes congregated and disseminated filth, food, and dangerous ideas. The poet's contempt is clear. Neumann puts it well: "Horace's objections are class-based aesthetics and social hierarchies dressed up as moral observations."[21]

Yet if we are looking in this poem for evidence of what Čulik-Baird calls "slave subjectivity," these lines may be one place to find it. "For the non-elite ... taverns and piazzas became the area in which their public life took place."[22] Almost invariably our literary sources are negative in their depictions of the tavern, treating the gambling and prostitution that took place there as its defining features.[23] "Just as I would not want to live among torturers, so I would not want to live among bars," declared Seneca (*Epistles* 51.4). Nonetheless, these were places in which the poor could escape the surveilling eye of their patrons, which offered relative safety in numbers in a world before electric light, and in which those without kitchens in their apartment blocks (*insulae*) could get food to eat. These were spaces of community in a Rome that feared and actively discouraged the *plebs* from meeting in large groups. The satirist Juvenal says that bars encouraged "equal liberty" (*aequa libertas*), which was, for him, an insult.[24] The *vilicus* in *Epistles* 1.14 despises the farm as "deserted and inhospitable" (*deserta et inhospita,* 19). You would rather be munching on your urban provisions with other slaves than enjoying the wholesome food of the country, alleges Horace (40). Yet the dream of traveling to the city, which is cast by the poet as some degenerate search for servile pleasure, looks very plausibly like a yearning for community. The *vilicus*

21. O'Neill [= Neumann] 1994, 226.
22. Toner 1995, 75.
23. Toner 1995, 67–83 is a good overview. A famous exception is the *Copa,* attributed to the young Virgil, which scorns the usual censure and lauds the seductive dancing of the female innkeeper.
24. *Satires* 8.177; for context, Uden 2015, 137–38.

may or may not, of course, be a real person, but there is nothing at all unlikely about the poet's description of the man's urge to travel. Readings that turn the *vilicus* into a metaphorical extension of Horace's own self miss an opportunity, even if fleeting and indirect, to hear some aspect of "slave subjectivity" in a text that otherwise keeps the enslaved in their place.

Just as powerful as the poet directly imposing his will on the *vilicus* is the poet's power of misdescription, his ability to represent the ordinary dreams and desires of the *vilicus* as "slavish" and thereby justify his own control. When the poet chidingly reminds the man that once he *wanted* to be sent to the country-side, he says (14–17):

> Tu mediastinus tacita prece rura petebas;
> nunc urbem et ludos et balnea vilicus optas:
> me constare mihi scis et discedere tristem
> quandocumque trahunt invisa negotia Romam.

> When you were a lowly slave you sought the countryside with silent
> prayer;
> now, as farm manager, you desire the city and the games and the baths.
> I, as you know, am consistent with myself. I depart with sadness
> whenever my hated business drags me back to Rome.

Because of his free status as much as his philosophical equanimity, Horace enjoys the "privilege of living unmasked."[25] He can be consistent with himself because he is not subject to another's whims, and he need not conceal his dissatisfaction out of fear that it could be perceived as ingratitude or subordination. But he can claim a greater power over the person that he owns. What does it mean, exactly, when Horace says that the *vilicus* longed for the countryside in "silent prayer"? The very notion invites suspicion, since the basic Roman assumption was that people would only pray silently or quietly for things too shameful to be spoken out loud.[26] "There is no reason to doubt that Horace is composing a humorous response to an actual request made by his overseer," says one scholar.[27] In fact the phrasing gives us ample reason to doubt. In being moved to the estate, the *vilicus* may have enjoyed some elevation in status, since he had been a *mediastinus,* a lowlier sort of slave, in the city. But Horace's most famous dialogue with a slave (*Satires* 2.7) ends with the threat to remove the insubordinate Davus to his Sabine estate, and being forced to take up agricultural labor is a stock punishment

---

25. I owe this formulation to our event's keynote speaker, James Johnson.
26. See e.g. Horace, *Epistles* 1.16. 57–62; Lucan 5.104–5; Persius, *Satires* 2.3–14; further passages at Kißel 1990, 297–99.
27. Guthrie 1951, 116.

for urban slaves throughout Latin literature.[28] Is this really what he wanted? If the *vilicus* was praying for anything, surely it was for freedom? If that was the man's silent prayer, Horace does not hear it – or, if he does, he has the power to misdescribe it.

FREEDOM AND RESTRAINT IN *ODES* 1.22

While *Epistles* 1.14 has been of interest primarily to scholars of Horace, *Odes* 1.22 (c. 23 BCE) is one of the Roman author's best-known lyric poems. The poem, addressed to the shadowy Aristius Fuscus (*fuscus* means "dusky" or "dark") hinges upon a strange, whimsical concept: the lover can suffer no harm. The concept had been developed by poets in the Hellenistic and late Republican eras as a light-hearted variation on the more sober philosophical notion in the ancient world that the wise man is invulnerable spiritually, if not physically, since his mind cannot be shaken by ordinary fears of danger or death. In a classic reading, Commager argued that Horace wrote *Odes* 1.22 to cast a wry, parodic eye on the fantasies of the love elegists, who had come to imagine themselves almost as sacred beings, sublimely invulnerable to external forces whenever they were ensconced in their amours.[29] Nobody would be so "barbarous" as to strike a man in love, claimed the poet Propertius (*Elegies* 3.16.14), fancifully. Horace creates a humorously literal version of this idea. Wandering just beyond the boundary of his rural estate, he tells us that a huge wolf appeared before him. But because he was singing the name of his beloved, Lalage, the wolf abruptly turned away and left him miraculously unharmed.

Horace surrounds this central anecdote with a quick narrative of extravagant journeys. Even in the most distant reaches of the known world, he says, the pure of mind will be impervious to harm. With its Sapphic metrical structure and prominent allusions to the two Sapphic lyrics of Horace's predecessor Catullus, *Odes* 1.22 is now most commonly read as a poem *about* poetry, celebrating the exalted status of the love poet and his ability to transcend ordinary boundaries of space and genre.[30] Yet *Odes* 1.22 is also very much about movement and mobility, and the ability of some travelers to enjoy special protections. Moreover, this freedom to travel is defined, as so often, against its ubiquitous opposite, enslavement, even if allusions to slavery are less immediately evident than they are in *Epistles* 1.14. Here is the entire poem:

28. Horace, *Satires* 2.7.118; cf. Fitzgerald 2000, 3: "One of the most dreaded punishments for the domestic slave was banishment to the country estate, or, worse, to the mill."

29. Commager 1962, 132–37.

30. McCormick 1973; Zumwalt 1975; Biondi 1995; Pucci 2005. On this reading, the encounter with the wolf symbolizes Horace's relationship with the wolf-like aggression of invective poetry: Davis 1987; Draper 2017. On the relationship between *Odes* 1.22 and its two most prominent Latin models, Catullus 11 and 51, see Ancona 2002, 168–76; Putnam 2006, 32–38.

Integer vitae scelerisque purus
non eget Mauris iaculis neque arcu
nec venenatis gravida sagittis,
    Fusce, pharetra,
	The man untouched in life and free from
	crime has no need of Moorish darts or bow;
	he does not need, Fuscus, a quiver heavy
	    with poisoned arrows,

sive per Syrtis iter aestuosas
sive facturus per inhospitalem
Caucasum vel quae loca fabulosus
    lambit Hydaspes.
	whether he will travel through the
	sweltering Syrtes or the hostile Caucusus,
	or whether through the regions licked by the
	    legendary Hydaspes.

Namque me silva lupus in Sabina,
dum meam canto Lalagen et ultra
terminum curis vagor expeditis,
    fugit inermem;
	For once I met a wolf in the Sabine woods,
	while I was singing of my Lalage,
	rambling, carefree, beyond my boundary.
	    It fled me, unarmed.

quale portentum neque militaris
Daunias latis alit aesculetis
nec Iubae tellus generat, leonum
    arida nutrix.
	It was a monster, of the kind not even rough
	Daunia breeds in its vast woodlands of oak,
	nor produced by Juba's land, that parched
	    nurse of lions.

Pone me pigris ubi nulla campis
arbor aestiva recreatur aura,
quod latus mundi nebulae malusque
    Iuppiter urget;
	Put me on barren plains where no tree
	is refreshed by the summer breeze,
	a part of the world oppressed with clouds
	    and dire storms;

pone sub curru nimium propinqui
solis in terra domibus negata:
dulce ridentem Lalagen amabo,
    dulce loquentem.
	put me under the chariot of the sun, too
	close to the earth, a land without homes;
	still I'll love my Lalage, laughing sweetly,
	    prattling sweetly.

Horace calls Daunia – a mythological name for the northern part of Apulia, Horace's birthplace – rough or "soldierly" (*militaris*, line 14), and readers have long noted military associations in the lands Horace mentions in his imaginary romp through the known world in stanzas one and two. The adventures he remembers, however, are no ordinary campaigns. Each contains an element of the marvelous. Traveling through the "sweltering Syrtes" conjures the image of the Stoic general Cato the Younger trudging through the deserts of North Africa in 47 BCE, an event that captured the Roman imagination almost immediately after it occurred, and which was later augmented with tales of giant serpents and mystical snake charmers in Lucan's epic *Pharsalia*. The "hostile" (*inhospitalem*) Caucasus was already immortalized as the rugged outpost of Greek myth, the place where Prometheus was chained to a cliff in primeval punishment. Pompey faced great difficulties there marching his army across its mountains and rivers in pursuit of Mithridates in 65 BCE, where he is supposed to have faced even Amazons in battle. Then, the "legendary" (*fabulosus*) Hydaspes is the Jhelum

River in modern-day India and Pakistan, the site of one of Alexander the Great's most famous battles, in which he crossed the flooded river and defeated King Porus and his elephants in 326 BCE. All these locations appeal to the mythical aspects of the Roman military imaginary.[31] In one of the major poetic models for *Odes* 1.22, Catullus boasted that his companions were so trusty that they would travel with him to far-flung India, Arabia, or the Nile, but also to more recent theatres of war, including the lands of the Parthians and to Britain, to see the war monuments of his contemporary Julius Caesar (11.1–12). *Odes* 1.22 lacks those touches of realism. The earlier poem tested the limits of the empire; Horace's poem tests the limits of the imagination.

The fact that these images of distant travel are addressed to a Roman man with a name that means "dusky" (*fuscus*) is inevitably suggestive. The word is used elsewhere of skin color: Hydaspes is the name of an enslaved man elsewhere in Horace's works, and he too is described as "dusky." The ethnic origins of Aristius Fuscus himself are irrecoverable, but Horace's fantasies of travel may nonetheless have been inspired by the exotic associations of his friend's name.[32] Other readers have also noticed the curious specificity in Horace's comparison of an Italian wolf to the kind of lion nurtured by "Juba's land." Lions were a prominent part of the political iconography of King Juba I of Numidia, and one scholar has even suggested that the geographical references of *Odes* 1.22 were intended as a compliment to Juba's son, Juba II, who had begun to move in elite cultural circles in Rome and had written an extensive geographical and ethnographic treatise on his homeland of Africa (the *Libyka*).[33] Travel involves crossing boundaries of identity as well as space, and there is an element of imaginary exchange of roles in Horace's fantastical journeys. The Roman, he says, will have no need for African bows, darts, or poisoned arrows, while traveling, if he is "untouched" in his morals. But why would a Roman be using such weapons anyway? For a people who fight with sword and shield, archery was the sign of the foreign opponent. Horace's predecessor Catullus imagined moving through the lands of the "arrow-bearing Parthians" (sagittiferosve Parthos, 11.6), but he never imagined shooting the arrows himself.[34]

31. On these associations with military campaigns, see Nisbet and Hubbard 1970, 266–68 and Olstein 1984. For Cato's march in the popular imagination in Horace's age, see Livy (*Periochae* 112) and Strabo (17.13.20), and soon after him, Velleius Paterculus (2.54.3). Pompey's struggle through the Caucasus: Plutarch, *Pompey* 34–35. Alexander's battle at the Hydaspes: Curtius Rufus 8.13–14; Arrian, *Anabasis* 5.9–19; Plutarch, *Alexander* 60.

32. "Perhaps Fuscus had some connection with India," Putnam 2006 suggests (at 133). He notes the parallel with *fuscus Hydapes* (*Satires* 2.8.14). For *fuscus* as a Roman name originally denoting skin color, see Kajanto 1965, 65.

33. Cairns 2012, 249–53. For the lion iconography of Juba I, see Roller 2003, 203–4; Cowan 2006 suggests a pun in *Odes* 1.22 between Juba's name and Latin *iuba* (mane).

34. As Sunil Sharma observed to me, these flights of fancy reflect a different kind of privilege of

Back at home, Horace pictures himself rambling (*vagor*) through his estate, a verb that highlights the freedom to be without aim or direction. Moving "beyond the boundary" of his property suggests some exciting transgression, a liberation from the limits that restrain lesser men. But it is also a reminder that he is a land-owner; the *terminus* is not only an abstract "limit" but the very real boundary that demarcates the edge of a parcel of land. In *Odes* 1.22, as elsewhere in Horace's po-etry, the fact that the Sabine villa was in fact a working farm is tactfully obscured; it is a "wood" (14), a sylvan retreat ripe for encounters like the one with the wolf.[35] That meeting is remarkably effortless: tension is immediately diffused, and an animal that could have threatened the life or livelihood of others spontaneously avoids the enchanted person of the confident man, convinced of his own moral goodness. Horace is carefree, and his unusual wording of that common idea un-derlines freedom from restraint: his "cares have been unshackled," he says (*curis ... expeditis*), using a verb that refers etymologically to the extrication of the feet from shackles or bonds.[36] Even the imperative verbs (*pone,* "put!") that begin each of the poem's two final, hyperbolic stanzas ironically highlight the impossibility of anyone giving Horace commands. Since he is not a soldier, or a prisoner of war, or a worker on his estate, or a slave, nobody will force him to travel where he does not want to go.

In *Odes* 1.22 as in *Epistles* 1.14, the freedom to travel is highlighted by im-plicit comparison with slavery. The poet's addressee Fuscus is a shadowy character. From references to him in other poems of Horace, we know that he was a close friend; that Horace valued his judgment on literature; and that he had a sense of humor. According to a later commentator on Horace's texts, he was also a writer of comedies, and perhaps also had some philosophical allegiance to Stoicism.[37] He was also, according to a different later commentator, a *grammaticus* ("the most outstanding *grammaticus* of that age") – that is, a schoolteacher, a profes-sion with a highly ambivalent social standing in Rome.[38] Moreover, *grammatici* could garner esteem as authors and intellectuals, but their lack of financial inde-pendence and association with the grubby realities of the schoolroom frequently counted against their social respectability. *Grammatici* were frequently foreigners,

---

the free, since when the *vilicus* in *Epistles* 1.14 dreamt of exotic incense and pepper (line 23), it was a mark of low taste, not imagination.

35. In reality, the Sabine farm was a "major agricultural establishment" (Leach 1993, 281); also Dang 2010, 107: "not a solitary and isolated place, but a property occupied by human interaction and economic production."

36. Nonius Marcellus p. 58, 4 (cited at Maltby 1991, 215): expediti et inpediti ex una propri-etate habent vocabuli causam, aut exolutis pedibus aut inligatis ("*Expediti* and *inpediti* derive the basis of the word from the same characteristic, from feet [*pedes*] either unbound or bound").

37. Poprhyrio on *Sat.* 1.9.60 (*scriptor comoediarum*). Gantar 1983 collects what is known about Fuscus; see in addition Harrison 1992 on Fuscus' possible Stoic connections.

38. Acro on *Sat.* 1.9.62 ("praestantissimus grammaticus illo tempore").

formerly enslaved, or both; Suetonius' surviving set of biographies of prominent *grammatici* shows that many formed close bonds with the political elite while still remaining, to various degrees, outsiders.[39] In Horace's only other poem addressed to Fuscus (*Epistles* 1.10), he counsels the man to avoid losing himself in the luxuries of the city, and brings him down to earth in the poem's close by reminding him of his status (or past status?) as a schoolteacher. Fuscus will not "dismiss" him without a "stern lecture," Horace predicts, wittily deploying the language of the ancient classroom, as Nisbet long ago observed.[40] Was Fuscus, like so many other *grammatici* of his age, a freedman? Did he have personal experience of slavery? The name had greater currency among freedmen than other common Roman *cognomina*.[41]

Clearer is the case of Lalage, whose name, amorously sung by Horace as he ambles through the woods, has an incantatory power over the wolf. The name, meaning "babbler" (from Greek λαλαγεῖν, "to babble"), is overwhelmingly attested among enslaved women. In Roman inscriptions, the earliest attestation of a "Lalage" comes from an inscription in the columbarium reserved for the staff of Livia, the wife of Augustus (the Monumentum Liviae). This Lalage seems to have been a freedwoman from the imperial household.[42] Among the graffiti in Pompeii, another Lalage is scratched on to the wall of a weaver's shop, together with a quantity of wool she could spin. Yet another Lalage, almost certainly a prostitute, is the subject of a line of erotic verse ("cruel Lalage, who [tells her lover?], 'I don't love you'...").[43] Elsewhere in Latin literature, Propertius speaks of an enslaved Lalage who is strung up by her hair and whipped (*Elegies* 4.7.45–6); Martial reverses the situation, and depicts a free Lalage beating her maid with a mirror because a hair has fallen out of place in her coiffure (*Epigrams* 2.66). Least clear is Horace's other *Ode* about a Lalage (2.5), since it has long been uncertain whether that Lalage is a young woman who has already been married, a young woman being sought for marriage, or a prostitute with whom the addressee desires some more lasting affair. Whatever her situation, she is an object of restraint: she is "not

39. On *grammatici* as both social outsiders and authors of works in low genres, see Uden 2020.

40. *Epistles* 1.10.44–6; Nisbet 1959, 74. Cairns 2012, 249 instead argues that Fuscus was one of Horace's patrons, who was "learned in letters" rather than a "schoolteacher." But that looser sense of *grammaticus* is very rare in extant Latin texts (Kaster 1988, 453–54), and other respected scholars and authors of Horace's era, such as P. Valerius Cato and Verrius Flacccus, were also schoolteachers.

41. Kajanto 1965, 65: "A cognomen like *Fuscus/a* was comparatively common in the sl/fr. class, 355 free, 43 sl/vf. or 11%, a figure which is greatly above the average of 5%."

42. *CIL* VI 3940a: *Liviae Lalage l(iberta)*. The name occurs eight times in surviving Roman inscriptions (Solin 2003, 615). See also Keith 2016, who helpfully explores correspondences between women's names in love poetry and the ancient epigraphic record (see at 73–74, 83 on the name Lalage).

43. *CIL* IV 1500; *CIL* IV 3042: crudelis Lalage, quae "non am[o" dicit amanti] (the line ending was suggested by Bücheler 1895, 439). A poem in the *Carmina Priapea* (*CP* 4) depicts another Lalage – presumably also a prostitute (Buchheit 1962, 74–76) – making a religious offering of sex manuals to the god Priapus.

yet strong enough to bend her neck and bear the yoke" (1–2), and Horace tells his addressee (perhaps himself) that he must wait until she seeks out a "mate" (*maritum,* 16) through her own sexual desire. "It is hard to see that this poem is set in a marital context of any kind," writes Harrison. It is likely that "Lalage is simply another in a sequence of non-marital affairs."[44]

What of the Lalage in *Odes* 1.22? With very few exceptions, scholars have treated her as a figment of Horace's imagination, or, more specifically, as a *symbol* of Horace's imagination. "Rare, of course, is the modern scholar who feels that Lalage represents a real person," wrote McClintock. "Her charming name and the lovely image of the last two lines indicate that she represents his poetry."[45] She is "not another one of Horace's lady loves, but the personified representation of his love song."[46] When Horace sings the name Lalage, writes Pucci, it is "a speech-act for the genre … *Lalage* is literally an onomatopoeic signifier for the sort of extemporaneous singing – "la-la-la-la-la" – that remains as familiar to modern ears as to ancient hearing."[47] Lalage may not be real, but her name is real, and elements of social reality still matter to the poem's interpretation. Her Greek name is a mark of otherness; she may be enslaved (compare Phyllis in *Odes* 2.4), a freedwoman, a prostitute, or some combination of those identities. Ancona writes that Lalage is "an extension of the poet/lover's own self," and yet that wording captures exactly one way in which scholars have described the master-slave relationship in Roman thought, according to which the enslaved become "extensions" of the bodies of the free.[48]

In underlining the centrality of human trafficking as a theme and plot device in Roman comedy, Amy Richlin points to the character of Hanno in Plautus' play *Poenulus* (The Little Carthaginian), who travels the ancient Mediterranean world and hires prostitutes in each port in order to try to find his lost daughters. "Behind every prostitute, an untold story," writes Richlin; "every one somebody's lost child."[49] Where was Lalage from? Horace imagines the man who is pure of heart moving through theaters of war with fantastical impunity, and then pictures himself rambling through his estate, thinking of a woman with an assumed name. What were her travels? She flits lightly in and out of the poem, a name on the poet's lips, with the power to avert a wolf. But if the name conjured the image

44. Harrison 2017, 83. For the opposing view that the name conceals a Roman woman "of respectable class," see Treggiari 1985.

45. McClintock 1975, 29, 32.

46. Zumwalt 1975, 429.

47. Pucci 2005, 10. A little-cited counterexample is Lucas 1938, who conjectures that Lalage was a "young freedwoman" (*une jeune affranchie*), identifying her with the Lalage of the Monumentum Liviae inscription.

48. Ancona 1994, 119. "Masterly extensibility" is the influential formulation of Reay 2005.

49. Richlin 2017, 363–64. She cites Hanno's questions at *Poen.* 109–10: "where was she from, what country, was she captured in war or kidnapped, who was her family line, who were her parents" (und' sit, quoiatis, captane an surrupta sit,/ quo genere gnata, qui parentes fuerint).

of a prostitute or freedwoman in the Roman mind, it was highly unlikely that Lalage was "untouched" (*integer*), the characteristic that the poet enthusiastically ascribes to himself. Only the free Roman male enjoyed that level of autonomy, and indeed only the free-born male could have promoted being unspoiled or untouched into a mark of virtue.[50] Seen in the context of social reality rather than poetic metaphor, the idea that a freeborn male might be *integer* is far from fantastical. Indeed, it is a basic assumption of elite Roman ideology: the free male is untouchable, while everyone around him is not.

MASKS AND MOBILITY

Manuela Coppola, in her chapter in this volume, explores the process of "Creolization" to which white travelers in the West Indies were thought to be susceptible in the eighteenth century. In a world of hybrid selves, she argues, whiteness itself became a category of identity that had to be achieved and performed, a mask that one had to wear. Similarly, the two poems of Horace explored in this chapter stage the identities of free and slave as sharply differentiated social roles, as masks with exaggerated features: the free poet is miraculously unscathed no matter where he goes in *Odes* 1.22, and the *vilicus* complains to his master in *Epistles* 1.14, longing to escape from agricultural drudgery to stereotypical pleasures and companionship in the city. In both texts, mobility and travel act as registers of social power. But for Horace himself, as for many of the schoolteacher-scholars and provincial transplants who were his peers, free and slave were enmeshed social positions, neither of them permanent or absolute. His own father had suffered through a period of slavery, and rather than obscuring that fact, Horace used his texts to illustrate how that shame could be converted into social capital. The declared "son of a freedman father," he meditated constantly on the meanings of freedom and slavery. Just as with comic actors on the Roman stage, then, Horace's readers must have wondered how much familial experience lay behind the enslaved characters in his own texts. In an age after Horace's death, the emperor Nero would notoriously don masks in tragic performance that resembled his own face: a reminder that stylization and literary performance can draw attention to the self as much as hide it.[51]

---

50. On *integritas,* see Kaster 2005, 134–48, who describes it as a "minimal" or "threshold" virtue implying "restraint, fixity, and scrupulousness." Other meanings of *integer* are also relevant to *Odes* 1.22: it can refer to virginity (being sexually "untouched"), and the collocation "untouched and untamed" (*integri et indomiti*) is used by Tacitus to describe freedom from the figurative slavery of Roman rule (*Agricola* 31.5).

51. Suetonius, *Nero* 21; see Cowan 2008. My thanks to the editor of this volume, Elizabeth C. Goldsmith, for her helpful suggestions, and to my companions in the Travel Literature Research Group at Boston University for keeping up the journey.

BIBLIOGRAPHY

Ancona, Ronnie. 1994. *Time and the Erotic in Horace's Odes.* Durham, NC.

———. 2002. "The Untouched Self: Sapphic and Catullan Muses in Horace, *Odes* 1.22." In *Cultivating the Muse: Struggles for Power and Inspiration in Classical Literature,* edited by E. Spentzou and D. Fowler, 161–86. Oxford.

Biondi, G. G. 1995. "Fusco e l'*integer vitae*: il programmo poetico di Orazio." *Paideia* 50:367–79.

Bowditch, Phebe Lowell. 2001. *Horace and the Gift Economy of Patronage.* Berkeley.

Bücheler, Franz. 1895. *Carmina latina epigraphica.* Leipzig.

Buchheit, Vinzenz. 1962. *Studien zum Corpus Priapeorum.* Munich.

Buzinde, Christine, and Iyunolu Osagie. 2011. "William Wells Brown: Fugitive Subjectivity, Travel Writing, and the Gaze." *Cultural Studies* 25 (3): 405–25.

Cairns, Francis. 2012. *Roman Lyric: Collected Papers on Catullus and Horace.* Berlin.

Carlsen, Jesper. 1995. *Vilici and Roman Estate Managers until AD 284.* Rome.

Commager, Steele. 1962. *The Odes of Horace: A Critical Study.* New Haven.

Cowan, Robert W. 2006. "The Land of King Mane: A Pun at Horace, *Odes* 1.22.15." *Classical Quarterly* 56 (1): 322–4.

———. 2008. "Starring Nero as Nero: Poetry, Role-Playing, and Identity in Juvenal 8.215–21." *Mnemosyne* 62 (1): 76–89.

Čulik-Baird, Hannah. 2020. "Staging Roman Slavery in the Second Century BCE." *Ramus* 48 (2): 174–97.

Dang, Karen. 2010. "Rome and the Sabine "Farm": Aestheticism, Topography, and the Landscape of Production." *Phoenix* 64 (1/2): 102–27.

Davis, N. Gregson. 1987. "*Carmina/ Iambi*: The Literary-Generic Dimension of Horace's *Integer vitae* (*C.* 1.22)." *Quaderni Urbinati di Cultura Classica* 27 (3): 67–78.

Draper, Kenneth. 2017. "Putting the Wolf to Flight: Horace's Disavowal and Deployment of Invective in *C.* 1.13–16 and 1.22." *American Journal of Philology* 138 (4): 641–72.

Dufallo, Basil. 2021. *Disorienting Empire: Republican Latin Poetry's Wanderers.* Oxford.

Fitzgerald, William. 2000. *Slavery and the Roman Literary Imagination.* CambridgeFraenkel, Eduard. 1957. *Horace.* Oxford.

Gantar, Kajetan. 1983. "Horazens Freund Aristius Fuscus." In *Festschrift für Robert Muth zum 65. Geburtstag am 1. Januar 1981 dargebracht von Freunden und Kollegen,* edited by Paul Händel and Wolfgang Meid, 129–34. Innsbruck.

Guthrie, Patrick. 1951. "A Note on Horace, *Epistle* 1.14." *Classical Philology* 46 (2): 116–17.

Harrison, Stephen J. 1992. "Fuscus the Stoic: Horace *Odes* 1.22 and *Epistles* 1.10." *Classical Quarterly* 42 (2): 543–47.

———. 2017. *Horaces: Odes Book II*. Cambridge.

Highet, Gilbert. 1973. "*Libertino patre natus.*" *American Journal of Philology* 94 (3): 268–81.

Hiltbrunner, Otto. 1967. "Der Gutsverwalter des Horaz." *Gymnasium* 74 (4): 297–314.

Isayev, Elena. 2017. *Migration, Mobility and Place in Ancient Italy*. Cambridge.

Johnson, W. R. 1993. *Horace and the Dialectic of Freedom: Readings in Epistles 1*. Ithaca, NY.

Joshel, Sandra R. 2013. "Geographies of Slave Containment and Movement." In *Roman Slavery and Roman Material Culture*, edited by M. George, 99–128. Toronto.

Kajanto, Iiro. 1965. *The Latin Cognomina*. Helsinki.

Kaster, Robert A. 1988. *Guardians of Language: The Grammarian and Society in Late Antiquity*. Berkeley.

———. 2005. *Emotion, Restraint, and Community in Ancient Rome*. Oxford.

Keith, Alison. 2016. "Naming the Elegiac Mistress: Elegiac Onomastics in Roman Inscriptions." In *Roman Literary Cultures: Revolutionary Poetics, Civic Spectacle*, edited by Alison Keith and Jonathan Edmondson, 59–88. Toronto.

———. 2021. "Women's Travels in Latin Elegy." In *Travel, Geography, and Empire in Latin Poetry*, edited by M. Y. Myers and E. Zimmermann Damer, 81–97. London.

Kenney, E. J. 1977. "A Question of Taste: Horace, *Epistles* 1.14.6–9." *Illinois Classical Studies* 2:229–39.

Kerber, Linda K. 2005. "Toward a History of Statelessness in America." *American Quarterly* 57 (3): 727–49.

Kilpatrick, Ross S. 1986. *The Poetry of Friendship: Horace, Epistles 1*. Edmonton.

Kißel, Walter. 1990. *Aulus Persius Flaccus: Satiren*. Heidelberg.

Leach, Eleanor Winsor. 1971. "Horace's *Pater Optimus* and Terence's Demea: Autobiographical Fiction and Comedy in *Sermo* I, 4." *American Journal of Philology* 92 (4): 616–32.

———. 1993. "Horace's Sabine Topography in Lyric and Hexameter Verse." *American Journal of Philology* 114 (2): 271–302.

Lucas, H. 1938. "Lalage dans Horace." *Revue de philologie, de littérature et d'histoire anciennes* 64:384–86.

Lyne, R. O. A. M. 1995. *Horace: Behind the Public Poetry.* New Haven.

Maltby, Robert. 1991. *A Lexicon of Latin Etymologies.* Leeds.

Marshall, C. W. 2006. *The Stagecraft and Performance of Roman Tragedy.* Cambridge.

Mayer, Roland. 1994. *Horace Epistles: Book I.* Cambridge.

McCarter, Stephanie. 2015. *Horace between Freedom and Slavery: the First Book of* Epistles. Madison, WI.

McCormick, Jane. 1973. "Horace's *Integer Vitae.*" *Classical World* 67 (1): 28–33.

McGann, M. J. 1969. *Studies in Horace's First Book of Epistles.* Brussels.

Muecke, Frances. 1979. "Horace the Satirist: Form and Method in *Satires* 1.4." *Prudentia* 11:55–68.

O'Neill, Jeanne N. [= Neumann, J.]. 1994. "Place in Horace: An Examination of Social Hierarchies in *Epistles* 1." PhD Dissertation, Harvard University.

Nisbet, R. G. M. 1959. "Notes on Horace, *Epistles* 1." *Classical Quarterly* 9 (1): 73–76.

Nisbet, R. G. M., and M. Hubbard. 1970. *A Commentary on Horace:* Odes, *Book 1.* Oxford.

Olstein, Katherine. 1984. "Horace's *Integritas* and the Geography of *Carm.* I.22." *Grazer Beiträge* 11:113–20.

Pryor, Elizabeth Stordeur. 2016. *Colored Travelers: Mobility and the Fight for Citizenship before the Civil War.* Chapel Hill, NC.

Pucci, Joseph. 2005. "Originary Song, Poetic Composition, and Transgression: A Reading of Horace, *Odes* 1.3 and 1.22." *Ramus* 34 (1): 1–21.

Putnam, Michael C. J. 2006. *Poetic Interplay: Catullus and Horace.* Princeton.

Reay, Brendon. 2005. "Agriculture, Writing, and Cato's Aristocratic Self-Fashioning." *Classical Antiquity* 24 (2): 331–61.

Richlin, Amy. 2017. *Slave Theater in the Roman Republic: Plautus and Popular Comedy.* Cambridge.

Roller, Duane. W. 2003. *The World of Juba II and Kleopatra Selene: Royal Scholarship on Rome's African Frontier.* London.

Scheidel, Walter. 2011. "The Roman Slave Supply." In *The Cambridge World History of Slavery, Volume 1: The Ancient Mediterranean World,* edited by K. Bradley and P. Cartledge, 287–310. Cambridge.

Shackleton Bailey, D. R. 2008. *Horatius: Opera.* Berlin.

Skalitzky, Rachel I. 1973. "Horace on Travel (*Epist.* 1.11)." *Classical Journal* 68 (4): 316–21.

Solin, Heikki. 2003. *Die griechischen Personnennamen in Rom: ein Namenbuch* (2nd ed). 3 vols. Berlin.

Toner, J. P. 1995. *Leisure and Ancient Rome.* Cambridge.

Treggiari, Susan. 1985. "*Iam proterva fronte:* Matrimonial Advances by Roman Women." In *The Craft of the Ancient Historian: Essays in Honor of Chester G. Starr,* edited by John W. Eadie and Josiah Ober, 331–52. Lanham, MD.

Uden, James. 2015. *The Invisible Satirist: Juvenal and Second-Century Rome.* Oxford.

———. 2020. "The Margins of Satire: Suetonius, *Satura,* and Scholarly Outsiders in Ancient Rome." *American Journal of Philology* 141 (4): 575–601.

Williams, Gordon, W. 1995. "*Libertino patre natus:* True or False?" In *Homage to Horace: A Bimillenary Celebration,* edited by Stephen J. Harrison, 296–313. Oxford.

Zumwalt, N. K. 1975. "Horace *C.* 1.22: Poetic and Political Integrity." *Transactions and Proceedings of the American Philological Association* 105:417–31.

Chapter 2

Crafty Crones in Disguise:
Two Examples from Premodern Literature

Sunil Sharma

MALE HEROIC CHARACTERS IN PREMODERN NARRATIVES routinely encounter a malevolent female force at a certain point in their wanderings as part of their obstacle course. A well-known example in epic literature is Odysseus's encounter with the monster Scylla and whirlpool Charybdis in Homer's classical Greek epic, *Odyssey*. Often the female appears in her true form, as in the case of the sorceress Circe in the same work, while in other narratives she first appears as a beautiful young woman and then reveals her true hideous appearance when spurned by the hero. The brief appearances of sorceresses, demonesses, and witches, who inhabit specific locales are episodes that represent obstacles on the journeys of male heroes. In some stories there is also a different kind of old woman or crone who is a master of disguise and masking: she is mobile rather than attached to one place. There are two prominent examples of such a characters in two premodern literary texts: one is Gabrina in Ludovico Ariosto's Italian epic-romance, *Orlando Furioso* (1532) and the other is Dhat al-Dawahi from the Arabic story of "King 'Umar ibn al-Nu'man" in the *1001 Nights*. I will study their roles in their respective narratives through the lens of travel, as their paths cross those of knights-errant or heroes, proving to be moving obstacles to be overcome by the latter. Both works have warring Christians and Muslims as the backdrop and draw imaginatively on legends, displaying a subjective memory of major historical events from the past – in one case the Muslim invasion of France during the reign of Charlemagne and the other the Crusades.

Let us first consider examples of an evil crone appearing as a beautiful woman in Persian and Indian epics. The first example is the witch whose killing is the fourth of seven trials of Rostam, the beloved hero of many adventures in the medieval Persian epic, *Shahnameh* (Book of Kings). On his way to the province of Mazandaran to rescue Kay Kavus, the foolish Persian king who is the prisoner of demons, Rostam comes upon a feast laid out in a sylvan landscape beside a stream. As he eats and sings to himself, he is heard by a sorceress (*zan-e jadu*) "who disguised herself as a young girl, as beautiful as the spring and lovelier than any painting."[1] Rostam is almost taken in by her, but when he offers thanks to

---

1. Ferdowsi 2016, 156.

God for the bounty, she at once reverts to her true form: "Suddenly there was a withered old woman in his lariat's coils, ugly, deceitful, and vicious,"[2] whom he slays on the spot. Similarly, in the Indian epic *Ramayana,* while in exile with this wife Sita and brother Lakshmana, the god-hero Rama encounters the demoness (*rakhshasi*), Shurpanakha, sister of the demon king Ravana. She represents everything he is not: "He was handsome, she was ugly.... He was young, handsome and honourable, she was old, cruel and deceitful. He walked the path of virtue, she was wicked. He was charming and refined, she was crude."[3] Shurpanakha makes a pass at him but fails to entice Rama; when spurned she curses him, thereby setting off a chain of events that culminates in a major battle.[4] In addition, she has her ears and nose cut off, as is the fate of many such evil female villains. The crones I will discuss have more involved roles in their respective stories.

Ariosto's *Orlando Furioso* is a verse romance based on chivalric legends about Charlemagne's rule and the Muslim/Moorish/Saracen invasion of France. It follows the wanderings of several heroic characters on both the Christian and Muslim sides, and in addition to the war between those two groups narrated in a mixture of epic and romance, includes the transcultural love stories of Orlando (Roland) and Angelica (princess of Cathay), and Ruggiero (Saracen) and Bradamant (Christian). The sinister crone Gabrina makes multiple appearances in this work, accompanying several male and female knights-errant on their various quests. She first makes an appearance without being named when Orlando, after a skirmish with some Saracens, chances upon Isabel, daughter of the Saracen king of Galicia, being held captive in a cave by a band of robbers. Isabel is watched over by an old woman until the merchant who has bought her takes her to "the Sultan in the East."[5] In the mayhem that ensues as Orlando liberates Isabel, "the old woman fled, clutching her hair and weeping, into the depths of the wild wood. After weary, arduous wanderings, terror hastening her heavy steps, she came upon a warrior by the bank of a river."[6] This is the Saracen female knight Marfisa, who in her wanderings sees "an old woman coming towards her; she was dressed in black, and was weary and prostrated from a long journey, but even more from sheer gloom."[7] Marfisa helps the old woman cross a river, and on the other side they encounter another knight, Pinabello, with a courtesan, who laughs at Gabrina's ugly appearance. Perceiving this as an insult, Marfisa fights Pinabello and defeats him:

2. "The witches and sorceresses in the *Shahnameh* are, on the whole, mirrors of their male magician/sorcerer counterparts," Pierce 2015, 361.

3. Valmiki 2000, 242–43.

4. In Kamban's Tamil version of the epic, she first appears as a beautiful woman and then changes to her hideous true self.

5. *Ariosto* 1983, 131 (canto 13, stanza 31).

6. *Ariosto* 1983, 132 (canto 13, stanza 41).

7. *Ariosto* 1983, 242 (canto 20, stanza 106).

> As victor of the encounter, Marfisa had the damsel remove
> her gown and all her ornaments, and gave them to the old
> woman, / bidding the crone dress up in the youthful attire
> and all the trinkets. She also had her take the palfrey which
> the damsel had ridden hither. Then she resumed her journey
> with the old crone, whose adornments only served to enhance
> her ugliness.[8]

From a sinister old woman, Gabrina is transformed into a dolled up traveling
monkey that accompanies its keeper to provide entertainment to others. Franco
Masciandaro explains how the code of chivalry motivates these knights even if
they would have liked nothing better than to be rid of her, "Her survival, we
gradually discover, is directly dependent on the knights' failure to go beyond
conventions and appearances. To them, in spite of her ugliness and her crimes,
she remains a lady to protect."[9] Ariosto is clearly mocking the earlier medieval
tradition of chivalry held so sacred by the knights.

As they travel further, Marfisa and Gabrina run into Zerbin, a Christian
knight and none other than the lover of Isabel, the damsel held captive in the
cave. Zerbin "simply had to laugh at the sight of the old crone – so glaring was
the contrast between her youthful dress and her hideously senile face."[10] At this
point, we get a further description of Gabrina:

> The woman (if her horny hide was anything to judge by)
> was more ancient than the Sibyl and, tricked out as she was,
> she resembled a monkey that has been dressed up for a joke.
> Right now she looked uglier than ever, now as she glowered
> and looked daggers.[11]

Zerbin mocks Marfisa for having such a ridiculous creature with her and equates
Marfisa's valor with the crone's beauty, thus provoking her to challenge him to a
duel: "If I lose to you, she must stay with me; but if I defeat you, I shall donate
her to you willy nilly."[12] But he is no match for Marfisa, and defeated, Zerbin
is forced to take Gabrina with him. It is only when Marfisa has ridden off that
Zerbin finds out from the crone who seeks to humiliate him that he had just
fought a Saracen woman – Marfisa had passed herself off as a man: Gabrina
"sniggered to herself; she was looking forward to needling him and making his

---

8. *Ariosto* 1983, 243 (canto 20, stanza 115-16).
9. Masciandaro 1980, 58.
10. *Ariosto* 1983, 243 (canto 20, stanza 119).
11. *Ariosto* 1983, 243 (canto 20, stanza 120).
12. *Ariosto* 1983, 244 (canto 20, stanza 125).

Figure 1. Gabrina, illustration by Gustave Doré. From the collection of the author.

life a misery."[13] Also, until this point Zerbin had believed that Isabel was dead; now he learns from Gabrina that she is alive but to his chagrin the old woman doesn't share any details with him.

13. *Ariosto* 1983, 244 (canto 20, stanza 131).

As Zerbin and Gabrina travel in silence, they meet yet another knight-errant, Hermonides of Holland, who attempts to seize the old woman. Mindful of his promise to Marfisa, Zerbin protects Gabrina, and when Hermonides does not desist, is forced to fight him. Hermonides is defeated and reveals Gabrina's backstory to Zerbin. Apparently, Gabrina was married to a nobleman named Argeus, but in a complex turn of events that involved his brother Philander, who spurned her sexual advances but then was forced to marry her when she tricks him into killing Argeus, the extent of her true wickedness is revealed. She then has Philander, who has been forced to marry her, poisoned by employing a "foxy physician," who is forced to swallow some of the same poison. Zerbin "if earlier he had found her tiresome and disagreeable, now he found her so loathsome he could not bear to look at her."[14] In turn, Gabrina's "loathing for him was not an ounce short of his for her – when it came to hating she gave even better than she got. Venom swelled her heart and showed on her countenance."[15] Again, it is the knight's code that keeps them together, "Ariosto, with the absolute control of the omnipresent poet, is consciously contrasting Gabrina with Zerbino in order to create a tension between her ever-changing schemes and the knight"s obstinate adherence to his code."[16]

In the next stage of their travel, Zerbin and Gabrina come across Pinabello's corpse. At this juncture, a further dimension of Gabrina's evil character is revealed, when the reader is informed that:

> Among her other faults, she was as greedy a woman as could be. / Had she had any hope of being able to steal them undetected, she would have taken his richly woven surcoat and his fine armour. What she could conveniently hide she took, while she smarted at having to leave the rest. Among her spoils was a handsome belt, which she took off him and girt about her waist between two skirts.[17]

14. *Ariosto* 1983, 254 (canto 21, stanza 70.

15. *Ariosto* 1983, 254 (canto 21, stanza 71). Immediately after this episode, at the beginning of the next canto, the narrator feels compelled to apologize for the negative portrayal of a female character by directly addressing his female readers: "You ladies who are gracious and kind to your true loves, and contented with a single passion – and without doubt in this you must be as one in a thousand – do not take amiss what I have been saying, when I was carried away against Gabrina; nor at the verse or two of censure I must still devote to the reprobate creature. / This is the woman she was, and as I have been bidden by One who has power over me, I am not evading the truth. But that does not tarnish the honour due to other women whose hearts are true.... For one woman whom I make bold to denounce in my poem – my story must have it thus – I am fully prepared to applaud a hundred others, and make their virtues more radiant than the sun." 255 (canto 22, stanza 1–3).

16. Masciandaro 1980, 57.

17. *Ariosto* 1983, 271 (canto 23, stanza 41–42).

This could be the description of a mischievous monkey, one who not only steals things but is waiting to break away from its captor. Looking for a chance to do more mischief, Gabrina goes to a nearby castle and tells the lord there that it was Zerbin who had murdered Pinabello; as a result, he is captured and chained in a cell.

As Gabrina herself flees "like a she-wolf who hears the pursuing huntsmen and hounds in the distance. / She was still wearing the dress and youthful ornaments which had been taken from Pinabello's pretentious damsel in order to clothe her," she encounters two Saracens: the champion Mandricard and Doralice, the daughter of the King of Granada: "The sight of this woman, who looked like a monkey, a baboon, tricked out in this youth raiment provoked Doralice and Mandricard to laughter." Mandricard takes Gabrina's bridle and her horse frightened by him "fled through the woods, carrying off the crone, half-dead with fright; he carried her over hill and dale, down paths straight and crooked, through ditches, across hillsides, at random."[18] But there is no getting rid of her and she is brought back to Zerbin, who has been rescued by Orlando in the meantime: "Zerbin had the old witch held while he decided what to do with her. He thought of cutting off her nose and ears, to make her an example to wrongdoers; then he thought it would be far better to let the vultures make a meal of her. In his mind, he turned over various punishments."[19] He in turn passes her on as punishment to Odoric, an ally who had betrayed him; "So many women, so many men had the crone deceived, so many had she injured, that her escort would not avoid challenges from knights errant."[20]

Zerbin has Odoric swear to keep Gabrina with him for a year and defend her from anyone who would want to harm her. Not surprisingly, she proves too much for Odoric and "they had gone only one day's journey when Odoric broke his pledge, and rid himself of Gabrina's constraining presence by throwing a noose round her neck and leaving her dangling from an elm."[21] Having proved to be an impediment in the journey of every knight she came into contact with, she is finally dispatched to the next world: "Justice is done by virtue of a negation of the chivalric ideals upheld by Zerbino and … Gabrina is punished for her crimes by one who has acted *contra ogni patto et ogni fede data,* and has refused to play the game imposed on him by Zerbino."[22] Gabrina's ignominious end is similar to that of the other crone discussed below, although the latter is a free agent and a stronger force of evil for several generations of Muslim princes and kings.[23]

18. *Ariosto* 1983, 277 (canto 23, stanza 95).

19. *Ariosto* 1983, 286–87 (canto 24, stanza 37).

20. *Ariosto* 1983, 287 (canto 24, stanza 42).

21. *Ariosto* 1983, 287 (canto 24, stanza 45).

22. Masciandaro 1980, 71.

23. Armida, a Syrian sorceress, can be mentioned here in the context of another Italian Renaissance epic set against the background of the First Crusade, Torquato Tasso's *Gerusalemme liberata*

In the *1001 Nights,* the longest story that the narrator Shahrazad stretches to one hundred nights is simply titled, "King 'Umar ibn al-Nu'man," and stands out as being different in several ways although it includes some of the usual tropes.[24] An independent story in the heroic *sira al-sha'biyya* genre, like many others it became attached to the larger collection at a later date. This romance-epic-saga features the multi-generational wars between Byzantine Christians and Muslims of the Arab regions of Iraq, Syria and Egypt, and includes the themes of travel, disguise, love, and conversion to Islam. Discussing the setting of the story, Wen-chin Ouyang explains,

> The landscape of the story, it is clear, derives not from the
> geographical boundaries defining the Islamic Empire, nor the
> history of the emergence of this Empire, nor the ethnic com-
> ponents of the Islamic communities, but from the landscape
> of its imagination, the way it imagines community as geneal-
> ogy, here of the Muslims, and against the "other," in this case,
> the Christians.[25]

Dhat al-Dawahi, an appellation rather than a name, which has been translated variously as Mistress of Calamities or Mischief, is a rather unusual character who plays a decisive role in the narrative. She is the crafty mother of Hardub, the Christian king of Caesarea. Not at all a sedentary character, she is constantly on the move, crossing the border between Byzantine and Muslim lands in various disguises with the single goal of annihilating the enemy. Her first appearance is in a bizarrely comical scene when she challenges her granddaughter Abriza (or Ibriza) to a bout as the latter is wrestling with ten female companions in the moonlight. Choosing to fight naked, the old woman is no match for the younger one. She "slipped out of her grip, but in trying to get free, she fell over with her legs in the air, showing her pubic hair in the moonlight. She farted twice, the first fart scattering the dust on the ground and the second raising a stench to heaven."[26]

The Muslim prince Sharkan, who is on a reconnoiter mission and spying on the female wrestlers, is unable to control his laughter at this grotesque sight and is soon captured.

While in gentle captivity, Abriza and Sharkan have no problems communi-cating with each other in Arabic. Abriza assures Sharkan that he is in her pro-

---

(1581). Although she is described as "a lady young of face, ancient in years" (270), she only appears as a beautiful woman who leads several men astray, including the Norman hero Tancred. She is first described in this way: "and all the Orient / no beauty to outshine her beauty shows. / Each darkest trick, each subtlest blandishment / a woman or a witch can ply she knows" (62).

24. *The Arabian Nights* 2010, 45–145 in the translation by Malcolm Lyons.

25. Ouyang 2000, 11; for an investigation into the origins of the story see Ouyang 2000, 8–11; also Christides 1962, 553–57.

26. *The Arabian Nights* 2010, 313.

Figure 2. Dhat al-Dawahi wrestling with her granddaughter Abriza. Kindly
supplied by Ulrich Marzolph from his archive of Persian lithographed illustrations.

tection and no harm will come to him. At a banquet, while her maids sing in
Greek, she wins him over with her Arabic song, and they recite poems to each
other. The Byzantine princess is shown to be conversant with the fine points of
comportment among courtly Muslims (*adab*): she speaks Arabic, can recite and
appreciate good poetry, and in the mold of many a *Nights* heroine, she falls in
love with the hero who has come from a kingdom far away and elopes with him.
However, their happiness is short-lived and back in Baghdad, while Sharkan is
away from the city, Abriza is raped by his father, the lascivious sultan ʿUmar, and
then subsequently murdered by a slave while trying to escape even as she gives
birth to a son. When her father learns about this, he is overcome by emotion and
swears to exact vengeance on ʿUmar, but his mother calmly assures him that she
will take vengeance in her own way: "I shall do something that will be beyond
the powers of the heroes and the men of wiles, something that people will talk of
in every region and place." Her first cross-border expedition takes place to avenge
the murder of Abriza.

    The detailed and burlesque description of Dhat al-Dawahi's character is wor-
thy of being quoted in full:

> That damned woman was a sorceress, skilled in magic and
> in lies, unchaste, wily, debauched and treacherous, with foul

breath, red eyelids, sallow cheeks in a dark face, and a body
covered with scabs. Her hair was grey; she was hunchbacked;
her complexion was pallid and her nose streamed with mucus.
She had, however, read Islamic texts and had traveled to the
Haram of Mecca – all this in order to study religions and to
become acquainted with the verses of the Quran. For two
years she had claimed to follow Judaism in Jerusalem in order
to possess herself of all the wiles of men and *jinn*. She was a
disaster and an affliction, with no sound faith and no adherence to any religion. It was because of his virgin slave girls
that she spent most of the time with her son Hardub, king of
Rum, for she was a passionate lesbian, and if deprived of her
pleasure for long, she would wilt away. If any slave girl pleased
her, she would teach her this art, crush saffron over her, and
fall into a lengthy faint on top of her as a result of the pleasure
she received.[27]

This hyperbolic portrayal of the crone's evil nature is of course meant to villainize
her as a member of the enemy community. Her being old is significant, as Amanda Steinberg explains in her analysis of the depiction of old women as opposed
to young virgins in medieval Arabic literature, "A common attitude that seems to
be shared by the *sīrah*s is that these powerful older women are intensely threat-
ening."[28] This particular kind of crone relies on her intelligence and position of
power to become a perpetrator of disastrous acts.

Dhat al-Dawahi's elaborate plan requires patience and involves infiltrating
the Muslim court in disguise; she commands her son:

Fetch me virgins with swelling breasts and then bring the wis-
est men of the age to teach them philosophy, courtly behavior
and poetry, and how to consort with kings. The teachers are
to talk with them on philosophical and religious subjects and
these teachers must be Muslims so that they can teach the
girls the histories of the Arabs, of the caliphs and of the old
kings of Islam. If this is done over a period of four years, then
we shall have reached our goal. You must show patience and
endurance, for it is an Arab saying that to wait forty years for
revenge is a very small matter, and by teaching those girls we
shall get what we want from our enemy.[29]

27. *The Arabian Nights* 2010, 433.
28. Steinberg 2018, 48.
29. *The Arabian Nights* 2010, 345.

King Hardub summons a group of Muslim scholars to train these girls; he treats them with great respect and pays them handsomely. Masking herself as a female ascetic, Dhat al-Dawahi offers the sultan the five "Muslim" girls as slaves, who impress him with their knowledge of Islam. As Peter Heath states, "She uses pious Muslim discourse, religious example, and saintly behavior, that is, the reverse of everything that she truly is, to achieve her goal."[30] We only return to this story a few nights later when the story of King ʿUmar's death is being narrated to his younger son. Over time, Dhat al-Dawahi successfully executes her plan to kill him by having him drink a poisoned jug of water that she pretends is blessed, before escaping back into Byzantine territory along with the five girls and another Christian girl, Sophia, the daughter of the king of Constantinople, who had also been captured by ʿUmar.

As the Muslims attack Byzantium, all the Christian powers in Europe unite to fight them. A devious military strategy is devised by Dhat al-Dawahi, who declares, "I shall show you a scheme that would baffle Iblis himself, even if he had all his ill-starred hosts to help him."[31] When this strategy fails, the Christians put their faith in a knight called Luqa ibn Shamlut, also known as "Sword of the Messiah," who is the male counterpart of Dhat al-Dawahi:

> He was an ugly man with the face of a donkey, the shape of
> an ape and the appearance of a snake. To be near him was
> harder to bear than to part from a beloved. His was the black-
> ness of night, the foul breath of the lion and the daring of the
> leopard.[32]

Luqa is killed by Sharkan and the Christians suffer a crushing defeat. Once again Dhat al-Dawahi proposes to go into the enemy camp, now to kill Sharkan, who had initiated the series of events by taking away her granddaughter.

This time Dhat al-Dawahi disguises herself as a male Muslim anchorite or Sufi:

> The old woman then took all the drugs she needed, put them
> in water and boiled them over a fire, dissolving their black
> core. She waited until the mixture had cooked and then
> lowered the end of a long kerchief over it. Over her clothes
> she put on an embroidered mantle, while in her hand she
> held a rosary. When this was done and she came out into the
> emperor's presence, neither he nor any of those sitting with
> him recognized her.[33]

30. Heath 2019, 211.
31. *The Arabian Nights* 2010, 423.
32. *The Arabian Nights* 2010, 425.
33. *The Arabian Nights* 2010, 432.

Along with a group of Syrian Christian merchants disguised as Muslims, she left for the enemy camp. There she further refined her disguise:

> She then put on robes of soft white wool and rubbed her fore-head until it acquired a large mark which she smeared with an unguent that she had prepared which gleamed brightly. She was a thin woman, with sunken eyes, and she now tied her legs, above the feet, and only untied the bonds when she had reached the Muslim army, by which time they had left weals, which she smeared with red juice. Then she told her compan-ions to give her a severe beating and put her in a chest. They were to cry aloud: "There is no god but God," and this, she assured them, would bring no great harm on them.[34]

Her elaborate masking of her true identity by displaying physical signs of cor-poral mortification fools the Muslims completely, to the point that Sharkan says to his brother, "This man has taken asceticism in this world to its furthest point and, were it not for the Holy War, I would stay with him and worship God in his service until I meet Him."[35] Dhat al-Dawahi explains to them that when she was a pilgrim in Jerusalem she was able to walk on water as a result of divine grace, and since then "my heart became hard and God afflicted me with a love of travel. I went to the lands of Rum [Byzantium] and travelled around its regions for a full year."[36] Masked as a male, she wreaks havoc among the Muslims, causing the defeat of their army and eventually the death of Sharkan, the prince who had ab-ducted her granddaughter at the beginning of the story. Her actions disrupt many lives and results in displacement: "Its heroes, Sharkan and [his half-brother] Daw' al-Makan, are condemned to aimless wanderings and adventures, during which the heroic transformation cannot occur and the individual, whether obtaining his objective or not, does not return to the collective to work towards building a 'nation'."[37] Two generations later, we learn that her great-grandson, Rumzan, Abriza's son by 'Umar ibn Nu'man, who had been brought up as a Christian by his mother's family, learns the history of his patrilineal heritage and accepts Islam. He and his nephew, Kana-ma-Kana, plot to take care of the unfinished business of Dhat al-Dawahi. She is lured to Baghdad on false pretenses and detained, and after three days she "was brought out wearing a red conical cap of palm leaves, covered with donkey's dung" and crucified on the city gate of Baghdad.[38] With this retribution, peace is established and Muslim rule is allowed to flourish.

---

34. *The Arabian Nights* 2010, 434.
35. *The Arabian Nights* 2010, 440.
36. *The Arabian Nights* 2010, 441.
37. Ouyang 2000, 13.
38. *The Arabian Nights* 2010, 613.

In the *Nights* story the boundary between the world of Christianity and Muslims is transgressed in several ways, for example, by people who can speak the other's language or mask themselves as their complete opposite. Nabil Matar states that "the depiction of Christians in the *Nights* shows a steady evolution, beginning in harmony, somewhere in the monastic cells of the Qur'anically admired monks, and ending in the conflict of a religiously contested Mediterranean."[39] Additionally, he notes that "[t]he conversion motif dominates the depiction of relations between Muslims and Christians"[40] in stories such as "Miriam the Sash-maker" and "Zahr al-Rawd." It must be noted that Saracens/Moors/Muslims are not portrayed in a particularly negative manner in *Orlando Furioso*,[41] and Gabrina is a Christian character, unlike Dhat al-Dawahi, who is from the community of the Other. When it comes to disguises in general in the *Nights*, according to Ulrich Marzolph, the most common forms of masking are when "Princes in quest of their beloved ... disguise[d] themselves as a merchant, dervish, or physician."[42] Also, young women disguise themselves as men in a number of stories. Then there are several female tricksters in the *Nights* and premodern Arabic literature, called *'ayyar*s like their male counterparts; Peter Heath explains: "One meaning of the root from which the word *'ayyar* stems is 'to frequently come and go, or wander.'"[43] Travel and mobility, prominent themes in the *Nights* in general, are not in the service of love and romance when undertaken by old female characters, but of violence and vengeance.

Studying the two characters comparatively, rather than individually as is usually done with such evil female figures, and using the motif of travel set against the background of a romanticized medieval Christian-Muslim encounter, allows us to consider them in multiple dimensions. When it comes to both physical descriptions of ugliness and mobility, Gabrina and Dhat al-Dawahi can be compared to the folkloric figure of the witch who flies around on a broom.[44] Both these women use poison at one point in their respective stories, a practice that

39. Matar 2008, 150.

40. Matar 2008, 151.

41. "The fact that modern scholarship is divided over the extent to which Ariosto's portrayal of the Saracen Other is positive and 'progressive' testifies to the complexity of the poem.... Saracen characters are often praised for their noble conduct. What is even more interesting is that some of Ariosto's early readers believed that that the poem had the potential to become a bestseller in the Arab world and in the Ottoman empire." Pavlova 2015, 478.

42. Marzolph 2004, 541.

43. Heath 2019, 207.

44. For a comparative study of witches in ancient Greek and Roman literatures, see Spaeth; additionally, "The Erictho of Lucan, and the likes of Horace's Canidia and Sagana, 'ugly/uncanny old women' (*Epod.* 5.98), bent wholly on evil, clearly foreshadow the aged, unnatural hags who will become so important a stereotype in European artistic, literary, and diabolical accounts of the witch," Watson 2019, 194–95.

is particularly associated with witches. In her study on vagrancy in Renaissance English literature, Linda Woodbridge writes, "One thing feared about witches that allies them again with beggars was their mobility – a supernatural mobility, in this case, that allowed them to fly, go out of their bodies invisibly, and travel anywhere, another crime against the ideology of homekeeping."[45] Not homeless or vagrant, Gabrina and Dhat al-Dawahi are actually women from elite backgrounds with family, but it is the inherent evil in their nature – although, in the case of the latter, it can be justified by the murder of her granddaughter – that mobilizes them. In fact, Dhat al-Dawahi "is queen mother but acts like a witch, is highly educated in religion but is totally immoral, very intelligent but cares only about trickery."[46] Crones are restless souls who are unable to remain stationary and calm, hence causing a great deal of mischief and destabilizing the lives of heroic figures in their pursuit of lofty goals.

Although female masking was also done by younger women, most notably in the crossdressing instances in some *1001 Nights* stories, with ugly crones in disguise the dramatic quality of the narrative is enhanced, as we saw above. In addition, their seniority endows them with "an immunity to the usual dangers to which younger and more attractive women would normally have been subject,"[47] expanding the narrative possibilities in all kinds of ways. The portrayal of them as burlesque and malevolent crones at the same time enshrines them in the narratives as stock characters, whose appearance both horrifies and entertains the reader. Their gruesome ends – one is hung and the other crucified – are also appropriate for the villainous roles they played in the narratives. The mobility that characterizes the roles of Gabrina in *Orlando Furioso* and Dhat al-Dawahi in the story of 'Umar ibn al-Nu'man showcases their dexterity with putting on various masks and disguises; although Gabrina does not fool anyone in the story with her appearance, Dhat al-Dawahi manages to fool everyone except the reader for a long period of time.

BIBLIOGRAPHY

The Arabian Nights: Tales of 1001 Nights. 2010. Vol. 1. Translated by M. Lyons. New York.
Ariosto, Ludovico. 1983. *Orlando Furioso.* Translated by G. Waldman. Oxford.
Christides, Vassilios. 1962. "An Arabo-Byzantine Novel 'Umar b. al-Nu'mān Compared with Digenēs Akritas." *Byzantion* 32 (2): 549–604.

45. Woodbridge 2001, 175.
46. Heath 2019, 213.
47. James Uden, written communication. I am grateful to him and Elizabeth Goldsmith for their comments on the first draft of my paper.

Ferdowsi, Abolqasem. 2016. *Shahnameh: The Persian Book of Kings.* Translated by D. Davis. New York.

Heath, Peter. 2019. "Dhāt al-Dawāhī and the Female *'Ayyār* in the *Arabian Nights.*" In *Tradition and Reception in Arabic Literature: Essays Dedicated to Andras Hamori,* edited by M. Larkin and J. Sharlet, 207–220. Wiesbaden.

Marzolph, Ulrich, and Richard van Leeuwen. 2004. *The Arabian Nights Encyclopedia.* Santa Barbara.

Masciandaro, Franco. 1980. "Folly in the *Orlando Furioso*: A Reading of the Gabrina Episode." *Forum italicum*, 14 (1): 56–77.

Matar, Nabil. 2008. "Christians in the Arabian Nights." In *The Arabian Nights in Historical Context: Between East and West,* edited by Saree Makdisi and Felicity Nussbaum, 131–153. Oxford.

Ouyang, Wen-chin. 2000. "Romancing the Epic: 'Umar al-Nu'man as Narrative of Empowerment." *Arabic & Middle Eastern Literature* 3:5–18.

Pavlova, Maria. 2015. "Orlando furioso." In *Christian-Muslim Relations, 1500–1900: A Bibliographical History,* edited by David Thomas and John Chesworth, 471–83. Leiden.

Pierce, Laurie. 2015. "Serpents and Sorcery: Humanity, Gender, and the Demonic in Ferdowsi's *Shahnameh.*" *Iranian Studies* 48 (3): 349–67.

Spaeth, Barbette Stanley. 2014. "From Goddess to Hag: The Greek and the Roman Witch in Classical Literature." In *Daughters of Hecate: Women and Magic in the Ancient World,* edited by Kimberly B. Stratton and Dayna S. Kalleres, 41–70. Oxford.

Steinberg, Amanda Hannoosh. 2018. "Wives, Witches, and Warriors: Women in Arabic Popular Epic." University of Pennsylvania PhD Dissertation.

Tasso, Torquato. 2009. *The Liberation of Jerusalem.* Translated by Max Wickert, with an Introduction and Notes by Mark Davie. Oxford.

Valmiki. 2000. *The Rāmāyana.* Abridged and translated by A. Sattar. New Delhi.

Watson, Lindsay. 2019. *Magic in Ancient Greece and Rome.* London.

Woodbrige, Linda. 2001. *Vagrancy, Homelessness, and English Renaissance Literature.* Urbana.

Chapter 3

How to Be Incognito:
Travel and Masking in the Memoirs of Sophia of Hanover

Elizabeth C. Goldsmith

WHEN SOPHIA OF HANOVER decided to write her memoirs in 1680, she had just celebrated her fiftieth birthday, and the recent deaths of two of her siblings had turned her thoughts to her own mortality.[1] Having lived in several different courts in Europe, and being related to most of Europe's royal houses, she was very aware of her official position on the family maps of history. Status and its maintenance through attention to protocol, etiquette, appearances, and concealment were all strong preoccupations that defined her character. At the same time, in setting out to write her life story she made it clear that she wanted to be able to tell it in her own unique way. While very aware of the extent to which her public identity was fixed in a web of dynastic politics, she would write a story of her life focusing on the episodes where she was traveling, far from her closest family members and exploring new ways of presenting herself to the world.

Born in 1630, Sophia was the twelfth child of the German Protestant prince Frederick V, sovereign of the region known as the Palatinate, and Elizabeth Stuart, daughter of King James I of England, and granddaughter of Mary, Queen of Scots. She was born and brought up at her parents' court in exile in The Hague in Holland, after her father was overthrown by the Catholic Hapsburg Holy Roman Emperor. Like her parents, who spoke and wrote to each other in French, Sophia's principal childhood language and the language of her education was French. She wrote her life narrative in French, dotting it with phrases in the several other languages that she knew: German, Dutch, English, Italian.[2] At The Hague she received an education in languages, philosophy, art, and music. When she was 19, she moved to Heidelberg to live with one of her brothers, who had recovered the family's sovereignty over part of the Palatinate. Because of her lineage on her mother's side, she would later in life be the first in line to the throne of England, despite the fact that she was the youngest of twelve children.

---

1. Elisabeth of Bohemia (1618–1680) and Karl Ludwig, Elector Palatine (1617–1680).
2. In addition to her memoirs, Sophia maintained a substantial correspondence with family members and with Gottfried Leibniz, most of it in French. See Van der Cruysse 2005, 129–31.

All of her older siblings had died or become ineligible. Sophia herself lived a long and healthy life, dying at age 83, on June 8, 1714, two months before the death of Queen Anne of Great Britain, and thus two months before she would have become Queen of England. Sophia's son George inherited the throne, becoming George I of England and the founder of the English House of Hanover, from whom the current royal family is descended.

Sophia's life was filled with travels. It was also a life that was imbued from childhood with the experience of displacement, of being out of place, and with an awareness of the important courtly skills involving feigning, hiding, veiling, masking, and strategic reserve. Even in her childhood and early married life, her cultural milieu was drenched in the practice of veiling and disguise. There were court performances and masquerades in which she performed, and extravagant allegorical portraits that her mother would commission, with a view to enhancing the family's political claims and personal mystique. In one giant family portrait Sophia is dressed as an angel flying over a host of her siblings surrounding a chariot driven by her mother and pulled by three lions, while her deceased father and brother look on from the clouds.[3] A more surreptitious and scandalous use of disguise was employed by Sophia's older sister Louise, who, in 1657, secretly ran away from the family, converted to Catholicism and became a nun. Louise was an accomplished painter, who had worked with Gerrit van Honthorst. Both artists produced portraits of Sophia in 1644, when Sophia was fourteen. In Louise's portrait, her sister is costumed as a Brazilian Indian.[4]

Perhaps fearing that Sophia would be tempted to disguise herself and run away like her sister had, her family married her off within a year after Louise's departure, to Duke Ernest Augustus Brunswick-Luneburg (1624–1705) of the House of Hanover.

Sophia describes her 1680 writing project simply as an act of "remembering the past, ... written for myself alone."[5] She had just been left behind at the court of Hanover while her husband was away on a trip to Venice. Unable – because not invited – to travel with him, she decided to spend her time writing an account of her past life. She did not publish the manuscript, but entrusted it to her close friend and interlocutor, the German philosopher Gottfried Leibniz, who had been living at the Hanover court. Leibniz transcribed the manuscript and

3. Gerrit van Honthorst, *The Triumph of the Winter Queen: Allegory of the Just*, 1636. Painting in the Museum of Fine Arts, Boston. For a discussion of this work and the family myths and ambitions it represents, see Goldstone 2018, 155–56.

4. Sophia and Louise's uncle, John Maurice of Nassau, had just returned to The Hague from Brazil, after having served as Governor of Dutch Brazil. His many stories and collection of colored prints of Brazilian animals, plants, and indigenous people inspired paintings and masquerades. See Francozo 2014. For a discussion of the popularity of costumes of New World indigenous people at masquerade balls, see Van Horn 2009.

5. Sophie de Hanovre 1990, 35. Translations are mine unless otherwise indicated.

Figure 1. Portrait of Sophia of the Palatinate in costume of Brazilian Indian, by Louise Hollandine of the Palatinate, 1644. Courtesy Wasserburg-Anholt Museum, photographer A. Lechtape.

added his own handwritten comments, praising what he termed its "apparently simple, but marvelously forceful style."[6] Rediscovered in the Hanover archives in a carton of curiosities including the memoirs of Frederick the Great (also written

---

6. Quoted in Sophie de Hanovre 1990, 19. Leibniz corresponded with Sophia and her daughter over many years, documenting their friendship and their discussions. See Strickland 2011.

in French), it was first published in 1879. In 1888 an abridged English translation was printed, and a German translation in 1913.[7] The first complete English translation was published in 2013.

In the opening lines of her memoir, Sophia offers the conventional apology for writing it, namely that it is something that she only wanted to do for her own pleasure and satisfaction, to pass the time while her husband was away, and that she had no interest in publication. As it happens his departure is for Venice, without her, and presumably to indulge his taste for Venetian pleasures (masking, performance, masquerade, beautiful women). As she remembers her own travels, she emphasizes how she had managed to negotiate these same interests herself. There is a competitive, playful tone to many of her anecdotes where she shows off her own knowledge and ability to evaluate the situations she encounters, and to indulge in, maybe give a different spin to, traveling practices that were more common for male travelers. Officially, Sophia's purpose in her travels was frequently to negotiate her family interests, advance marriage settlements for her nieces, nephews, and her own children, or establish cultural exchanges that would enhance the international prestige of the Hanoverian court.[8] On a more personal level, Sophia's travels inspire her to reflect on the challenges involved in representation and diplomacy, in always being viewed as a public personage. She refers frequently to her practice of traveling incognito and the purposes it served. She also muses on the nature of disguise, on how outer appearances are almost always deceptive, describing her own ability to unmask and see through the most carefully constructed disguises. In the process of remembering her role as an informal diplomat on her travels, Sophia also explores her own feelings about playing this role, and in doing so she reflects on incognito not just as a practice but as a repeated experience of her own subjectivity. She describes herself not just as traveling incognito, but as *being* incognito.

It is interesting to think about how she set up the presentation of her memoir manuscript, confiding it to Leibniz, her friend, confidant, partner in conversation and correspondence.[9] In fact, Sophie's inclination to view masking and the practice of incognito as a way of being may be connected to her conversations with Leibniz about the nature of the soul and his concept of animal and human nature. Leibniz was fond of using theatrical metaphors in his scientific and philo-

7. See Van der Cruysse's introduction to Sophia of Hanover 1990, 18–24.

8. On the different roles played by royal women travelers in building court society in the seventeenth century, see Nolde 2008.

9. By writing her memoir with only a limited audience in mind, Sophia is approximating her narrative to a letter, and maintaining its personal, conversational quality. In this way, like a letter, her memoir can be intimate, confidential, and sealed from public view, while also proposing to share "truths" that are veiled from others. Also like letters, her memoir seems to give readers an advance taste of future revelations. See Raycraft's comments in this volume, on how Durand-Fardel's letters "serve as a prelude to conversations she plans to have when she returns."

sophical explanations. One that he returned to several times in his letters was the commedia dell'arte character of Harlequin, master of disguise, whose "true" identity could never be fully revealed even when he is trapped and stripped on stage, for each layer of costume that is taken off only reveals another one underneath.[10]

Sophia's account of her life is largely a travel narrative, and one that describes many of the reasons that a woman of her era and rank might spend a good part of her life on the road. Her travels were visits, first to courts inhabited by her large and widely scattered family, and then to more distant courts in France, Italy, and England, where she would represent the two dynasties that she belonged to: her birth family of Palatine or her married one of Brunswick-Lunebourg. Masking and traveling incognito, under an assumed name and without outward show of her noble identity, was a way to travel more easily, at less expense, and it eased Sophia's encounters with the prominent people she was interested in on her travels. These incognito appearances did not in fact fully disguise her identity, but they gave her more freedom of movement and expression, potentially liberating her to be more sincere in her interactions.

The second half of the seventeenth century saw incognito established as a familiar diplomatic practice, and a socially acceptable way to escape the burdens of rank and protocol.[11] It was "just like an actor changing masks," in the sense that all viewers accepted the fiction, while knowing full well that the same actor remained behind the mask.[12] For royal personages traveling incognito, the practice could effectively muzzle any talk of state or business affairs. It could also simply function to downplay the significance of one's presence at a foreign court, giving the traveler more freedom of movement and expression. As James Johnson observes in his study of the practice in Venice, "'anonymity' served its purposes without hiding identity."[13] Incognito travelers, dispensing with ritual social formalities, could gain the confidence of their hosts more quickly. After Sophia's return home she might be contacted by a foreign court she had visited and asked, for example – as happened after her first visit to Louis XIV's court – to report on candidates for a marriage or help mediate an alliance. Her memoirs describe her voyage to Strasbourg in 1671 (four weeks after giving birth!), to accompany her brother and her niece Elisabeth-Charlotte, to negotiate Elisabeth-Charlotte's marriage to Louis XIV's brother Philippe d'Orléans.

Another function of incognito that Sophia seems to particularly enjoy is that it helps her to more easily see the truth behind appearances. Accustomed to being constantly observed at her own court, her travels incognito enable her

10. On Leibniz's use of metaphors of masking and theatre see Becchi 2016. Becchi notes (406) that Leibniz refers to the mask of Harlequin and its endless stripping off in a letter to Sophia.

11. For a general discussion of the practice see Barth 2014.

12. Lemée 2020, 16.

13. Johnson 2011, 139.

to become more viewer than viewed. In disguise, unencumbered by the need to focus on protocol and ceremony, she can better critique the efforts of others to present themselves in a particular way. On her travels, Sophia frequently invokes encounters with others who are disguised, masked or otherwise interacting with her via some form of veiling. It was a common trope in travel accounts written by men to compare the beauty of women in different countries, symbolically unveiling those who try to evade the traveler's gaze. Several times on her own itinerary, Sophia arranges to view groups of young women so that she might comment on their beauty. On her trip to Italy in 1664, she attends a ball for this purpose in Milan, and in Bologna, a beauty pageant is arranged for her. In Venice she is taken to a convent to admire the beauty of girls whose families, she is told, want to keep them out of sight until they are married. In all these instances Sophia's perspective is one of a viewer eager to see the "truth" behind a reputation for beauty that has been circulated, either through portraits or verbal description.

Sophia takes a similarly demystifying approach to the beauty contest implicit in royal portraiture and engravings of female royals. She describes how portraits that had been done of herself in her own youth were flattering, while in person she had been deemed "skinny and ugly" as a child.[14] When she travels with her mother to The Hague to greet the Queen of England in 1642, she is surprised to see that Henrietta Maria and her companions did not resemble their portraits:

> The fine portraits by Van Dyck had given me a lofty idea of
> the beauty of all English ladies. I was therefore surprised to
> discover that the queen, so beautiful on canvas, was actually a
> short woman … with long wizened arms, crooked shoulders,
> and teeth protruding from her mouth like ravelins from a
> fortress.[15]

She often reflects on how one forms impressions of people through the ways they are first represented in allegorical or romanticized portraits or via encounters that are incognito. Her thoughts on the practice of portraiture as a vehicle for introducing potential candidates for marriage seem to question – and explore – whether these outer signs have similitude with the subjects they represent. In the marriage market, she concludes, viewers are overly reliant on portraits to make decisions.[16] And while she enjoys the privileges of her own incognito, she regularly unmasks others – in her own written portraits of purportedly beautiful

14. Sophia of Hanover 2013, 38.
15. Sophia of Hanover 2013, 42.
16. For a detailed discussion of how portraiture in this period could be viewed as a form of incognito, see Velissariou 2002.

women, for example. In this way, Sophia's practice of incognito leads her to examine the whole experience of seduction and attraction.[17]

The first voyage incognito that Sophia describes in her memoir was to Venice where, sixteen years earlier, her husband *had* invited her to join him. She emphasizes, in fact, that she made the trip by herself, that is, unescorted by any male relative and accompanied by her own chosen retinue of servants, squires, and musicians for the trip across the Alps. She insists on staying at inns rather than being received by resident nobility en route, much to the frustration of some in her entourage. When she arrives in Venice, a place so beloved by her husband, Sophie writes that she was struck by nothing so much as the fact it seemed never to be as it first appeared – the women were not so beautiful as reputed, efforts to entertain her seem excessive and forced, the perpetual masking puts her on edge, and when her husband asks her if she doesn't find Venice beautiful she replies that no, to her it seems depressing, "very melancholy"[18]. She falls sick and feverish from the bad air, declaring "Italian customs no more suited my mood than the air did my bodily temperament."[19] Everything in her experience of Venice – that epicenter of incognito culture! – seems off: her entourage suffers a serious carriage accident, she attends a debate at an academy where the topic was: "if you had to go mad, which type of madness would you choose?" and out of every social interaction, whether it was conversation in the street, visiting a convent, a church, or attending a concert, she notices that Venetians are intent only on arranging amorous encounters. "You can imagine," she writes, "how a German woman like me felt out of place in a country where they think only of lovemaking, and where ladies would think themselves dishonored if they don't have lovers."[20]

Her husband proceeds to introduce her to other Italian cities – where each time she seems to be struggling to find a level of incognito that is more comfortable, somehow more authentic: Milan, where they both attend a masked ball and together admire the beauty of the women, and where she decides in order to be more comfortable she would not wear a fully masked costume; Parma where she wanted to remain incognito but where the duke insisted on a magnificent reception for her; and finally Rome, by which time their incognito entourage has swollen to 200 people.

The visit to Rome in 1664 held a particular significance for both Sophia and her husband, for it was the residence of Maria Mancini Colonna, a woman with whom Sophia's husband was infatuated. She was a niece of Cardinal Mazarin,

---

17. Unmasking conventional standards of beauty is a theme returned to by other early women travelers discussed in this volume. See the essays by Raycraft and Coppola.

18. Sophie de Hanovre 1990, 80.

19. Sophie de Hanovre 1990, 91.

20. Sophie de Hanovre 1990, 93.

who had married into Roman nobility and gained an international reputation for her patronage of the arts, her engaging and cultivated conversation, and her attractiveness. Sophia was particularly curious to see this woman, who had a few years earlier conducted a celebrated romance with the young Louis XIV, and who now continued to receive the adoring attention of men, including Sophia's husband. In fact, in deciding to write her own memoirs fifteen years later, Sophia would make reference to the recently published memoirs of Maria Mancini and her sister Hortense, both of whom had run away from their husbands and written about their adventures. In her prefatory statement, Sophia asserts how her own story will be different:

> As at the age that I find myself there is no better occupation
> than to remember times past, I think I can satisfy this need
> without resembling, in this writing which is only for me, a
> heroine of a novel. I do not wish to imitate those romantic
> ladies who made spectacles of their lives with their extraordi-
> nary conduct.[21]

Hortense Mancini had published her 1675 memoir and signed it, characterizing her life in the opening pages as resembling a novel (precisely what Sophia says she wants to avoid). Maria had published her 1677 memoir anonymously, but arranged for its printing and circulation with the help of none other than Sophia's husband, the Duke of Brunswick-Lunebourg, to whom the 1678 edition of the book was dedicated.[22] Sophia's memoir opens describing herself left at home in the winter of 1680–81, while her husband makes a trip to Venice during carnival season, where, as Sophia knew, in the old days he would rendez-vous with Maria Mancini Colonna.

As she describes her 1664 trip to Italy with her husband, she seems to be seeking a place where elite figures manage to live with just the right measures of ceremony and naturalness. Rome and Venice were decidedly not such places, but in Florence, she admiringly observes the behavior of Prince Leopold of Medici, who would later be named Cardinal and was in the habit of dressing like a priest. She is alerted to this by another courtesan in case she did not recognize him in these clothes, but she already had:

> I had already recognized him by his manner and his noble
> demeanor. ... I found that he was neither too formal nor too

---

21. Sophie de Hanovre, 35.

22. For a summary of the publication history of these memoirs see Nelson in her introduction to Mancini 2008, 9–12. On the different ways in which the two Mancinis and a cluster of other women contemporaries orchestrated the circulation of their autobiographies, see Goldsmith 2001.

> familiar in all that he did. He lived very agreeably with his
> noble status.... I was not overwhelmed by excessive civility as
> I had been elsewhere.... I felt so satisfied when I left Florence,
> I found it to be the most agreeable place I had seen in Italy.[23]

"He lived very agreeably with his noble status" – this observation becomes a kind of personal aspiration for Sophia, who on her continuing travels tries to achieve a similar kind of comfort with her own always encumbered, often disguised social self. For her, some level of incognito is required when she is anywhere except perhaps her own rooms and garden. In this sense traveling incognito becomes for her a series of experiments in finding the best balance of naturalness and artifice, outer demeanor and inner thought, a perfect metaphor for the ever-present necessity of self-concealment that anyone – perhaps especially a woman – of her rank would have considered necessary for both happiness and survival.

In 1679 Sophia traveled to Paris and the court of Louis XIV, initially with the idea that she was trying, informally and incognito, to arrange a marriage for her daughter Sophie-Charlotte to the king's son. But by the time she arrived in France it was clear that another marriage was already being arranged for the Dauphin. Her visit then had to take on other purposes, as did her incognito. Before going to Paris, she first paid a visit to her sister Louise, who by now was abbess of the Cistercian convent of Montbuisson. For this visit she is incognito, but only barely, traveling in what she calls a "country outfit."[24] Both sisters, then, greet each other in a kind of simple incognito that each has assumed – one dressed in her country clothes, traveling under the name Madame Osnabruck – and the other having taken the nun's habit along with a new name – Maria – to mark her religious conversion. At the abbey she is also reunited with her niece, Elisabeth Charlotte, and she meets her niece's husband Philippe, brother to Louis XIV. They make it clear that Sophia will be welcome at court simply as a representative of the court of Hanover and her extended family, and that her incognito will be useful in that role. Sophia tells them that her husband had wanted her to just stay at the convent, once there was no longer any specific diplomatic purpose to her visit. But Philippe would have none of it, insisting that she come into Paris "to see everything," as he put it.[25] So she is guided by Philippe, for whom the pleasures of disguise and masquerade extended well beyond any overtly diplomatic interests – he enjoyed masquerade, and was well known for his fastidious attention to fashion, jewelry, and cross-dressing.[26] His homosexuality and same-sex romances

---

23. Sophie de Hanovre 1990, 103–5.
24. Sophie de Hanovre 1990, 141.
25. Sophie de Hanovre 1990, 250.
26. For a discussion of the fashion of cross-dressing and masquerade at the court of Louis XIV, see Cohen 1999.

were well known and accepted at the French court. Sophia may have wondered how she was going to respond to this man who had married her niece, but she reports that she liked him immediately, and he quickly took her under his wing.

He showed her that being incognito could protect her, in a way, from making gaffes or doing anything that would embarrass her family. "The Prince," Sophia writes, "gave me a most obliging welcome, and acted as though he had known me his whole life. As I embraced my sister he walked ahead with his daughter, and I followed after a few moments with Madame, who was holding me tightly next to her heart."[27]

Philippe is interested in her choice of incognito and tells her that when they get to his own residence in Paris, she can retain the simplicity of it: "He seemed pleased with my incognito and said if I want to keep it at Palais Royal, I only had to put on a black shawl. I accepted the challenge."[28] When they arrive at Palais Royal Philippe immediately wants to show her the clothes and jewelry he has given his daughter by his first marriage, Marie-Louise d'Orleans, for her impending wedding to the king of Spain. In her description of this she emphasizes that Philippe wanted her to know the real value of these items, not letting her presume that the gold filigree on the dress was real gold, for example, but also explaining what gave real value to the setting of pearls. "As he has a real talent for these things," she writes, "he also looked at my own jewels and told me how he would like to alter them in a different style, which he very carefully ordered to be done."[29] After this kind of initiation scene he advises her on how she should appear before the king, telling her, "the king my brother will not be annoyed to see you incognito," and advising her that in this way she could also observe the marriage proxy ceremony of his daughter without being noticed. He spends time with her arranging for the clothing that she and her ladies would wear, then Sophia returns to the convent for three days, before returning to Paris and to Philippe d'Orléans' attentions to the costumes that by then were ready for her. They go to the theatre, where she says, "I was so incognito that I was loudly announced with the words: Make way for Madame d'Osnabruck!"[30] She paid a visit to her niece and Philippe in their private rooms late in the evening and noticed he was embarrassed to be seen in his evening gown. "I made him feel better by adjusting his jewels and his nightcap ribbon," she writes.[31] The whole visit is filled with details of this nature that emphasize clothing, attention to appearances, disguise, but all permeated with a sense that she is learning how to use them in a new way that is comfortable and familiar. Almost everywhere she is escorted by "Monsieur." Her visits to court alternate with little breaks to be with her sister in

27. Sophie de Hanovre 1990, 142.
28. Sophie de Hanovre 1990, 142.
29. Sophie de Hanovre 1990, 143.
30. Sophie de Hanovre 1990, 146.
31. Sophie de Hanovre 1990, 147.

her convent, as well as outings to Philippe's country chateau of St. Cloud. On one visit to St. Cloud her carriage overturns just as she arrives at the entrance, leaving her bruised and humiliated. Philippe, ever the good friend, rushes out and picks her up, taking her to the room he had chosen for her overlooking his gardens.[32] When she is later taken to visit Versailles, she declares "I would prefer St. Cloud, if I had to choose."[33]

In the background of her visit are the elaborate engagement ceremonies with Spanish emissaries to the court in preparation for the departure of the King's niece for Spain to join her new husband. Just before this departure the young princess summons Sophia to be present while her father shows her the jewels she has received from the Spanish king along with his portrait that has been sent to her. The portrait is not attractive. Marie-Louise was miserable. Sophia tries to console her with the observation that is it not well painted and may not be a good likeness, but the princess says to her bluntly, "they say that he resembles that ugly magot the duke of Wolfenbuttel."[34] It is a moment of truth, all masks are dropped, and the princess pointedly violates protocol by seating herself on the same kind of stool that Sophia has been given. Sophia's account of Marie-Louise's departure for Spain to join her ugly husband dwells on the family's painful goodbyes. Writing this account over a year later, she would have known that the Spanish marriage was not developing into a happy one.

As she prepared to leave France, Sophia reported in a letter to her brother how Philippe and her niece had managed to transform her informal and aborted diplomatic visit into one where she was gracefully welcomed into the French royal family:

> Madame was careful to treat me in my incognito in such
> a way that the royal princesses and electresses will have no
> cause for complaint. This noble princess has always treated
> me without ceremony, in the German style, and Monsieur
> even escorted me in front of the Spanish Queen [Louis XIV's
> wife Maria Theresa] so that there would be no prejudicial
> comments in Germany. Everyone says that he would not do
> the same for others, as he has a special care for me.... I think
> that Monsieur has understood that he risks nothing with me,
> that I understand his concerns as well as my own. If I had
> to enumerate the praises that I have for that prince I would
> never be finished; I think that Madame is one of the luckiest
> women in the world.[35]

32. Sophie de Hanovre 1990, 154–55.
33. Sophie de Hanovre 1990, 157.
34. Sophie de Hanovre 1990, 151–52.
35. Sophie de Hanovre 1990, 258.

Sophia's voyage to France was a turning point in her discovery of her own taste, in the ease with which she could move between different places and companies, and in her approach to the practice of incognito, which she learned to absorb into her style of life and use with a flexibility that was not her habit before. Incognito has become a way of *being* in her travels, but there are grades of it, and when she finds the optimal level this is when she feels most herself. The French voyage was not one where she had accomplished any particular diplomatic tasks for her family. But when she is reunited with her husband, who had wanted her to simply stay at the Montbuisson convent, he tells her that he is "very satisfied by my conduct, and that he found that I had done very well at the court of France."[36] After returning to Hanover from France she took over the design and construction of the gardens at her palace at Herrenhousen, for which she engaged a French landscape gardener and which contributed to her becoming known for the "French" style of her court – in fashions, which her niece wrote to her about regularly, in dance, and in other court festivities, including frequent masquerades.

Sophia's reflections on incognito travel, and her experiments with it, lead her to develop a measure of personal independence, and eventually a kind of freedom to discover and express her own character. Traveling incognito can be in her mind a virtue, and almost a way of living that gives her a deeper sense of freedom than simply a freedom from the material trappings of her rank. Her memoir, inspired by an episode of tension in her marriage and thoughts of her own mortality, records her discoveries, on the road, of the every-present importance of the mask. Like Leibniz's metaphor of the veiled Harlequin, Sophia acknowledges that a full "unwrapping" of identity is never possible.

In conclusion, I want to return to Sophia's initial explanation of her reasons for writing, and her decision to entrust her manuscript to Leibniz. She asks that it remain unpublished, unknown, in fact incognito, in the sense that even as its author wished to remain masked, officially unrecognized, at the same time her identity was transparently clear to any reader. It seems impossible that she would not have envisioned some type of circulation of the memoirs that Leibniz would oversee. Her whole relationship with him was based on precisely this kind of private circulation of ideas and conversation with a select public through letters. Her "incognito" manuscript enables her to be a writer who does not put herself out into the world but chooses an eminent philosopher as her principal reader, a friend and editor already her intellectual patron through their correspondence. We don't know what they said to each other about this manuscript but we do know that he copied it and made notes on its value. Perhaps pointing to another type of incognito in the substance of Sophia's writing, he writes: "The style seems

36. Sophie de Hanovre 1990, 167.

simple, but it has a marvelous power.... Even when it *seems* that she is describing only ordinary things, she elevates them with turns of phrase that inspire a solid reflection on humanity."[37]

BIBLIOGRAPHY

Barth, Volker. 2014. "Les visites incognito à la cour des Bourbons au XVIIIe siècle." In *Voyageurs étrangers à la cour de France, 1589–1789*, edited by Caroline zum Kolk, Jen Boutier, Bernd Klesmann and François Moreau, 323–37. Rennes.

Becchi, Alessandro. 2016. "Leibniz' Harlequin and the Theater of Organic Bodies." In *Für unser Glück oder das Glück anderer. Vorträge des X. Internationalen Leibniz-Kongresses Hannover*, edited by Wenchao Li, vol. II, 401–416. Hildesheim.

Cohen, Sarah. 1999. "The Masquerade as Mode in the French Fashion Print." In *The Clothes that Wear Us: Essays on Dressing and Transgressing in Eighteenth-Century Culture*, edited by Jessica Munns and Penny Richards, 174–207. Newark, NY.

Francozo, Mariana. 2014. "Global Connections: Johan Maurtis of Nassau-Seigen's Collection of Curiosities." In *The Legacy of Dutch Brazil*, edited by Michiel Val Groesen, 105–24. New York.

Goldsmith, Elizabeth C. 2001. *Publishing Women's Life Stories in France: From Voice to Print*. Aldershot, UK.

Goldstone, Nancy. 2018. *Daughters of the Winter Queen*. New York.

Johnson, James. 2011. *Venice Incognito: Masks in the Serene Republic*. Berkeley and Los Angeles.

Lemée, Emmanuel. 2020. "The Language of *Incognito* in Late Seventeenth-Century Diplomacy," *Legatio* 4:15–36.

Mancini, Hortense, and Marie Mancini. 2008. *Memoirs*. Edited by Sarah Nelson. Chicago.

Nolde, Dorothea. 2008. "Princesses voyageuses au XVIIe siècle: Médiatrices politiques et passeuses culturelles." *Clio: Histoire, femmes et sociétés* 28:59–75.

Probes, Christine McCall. 2018. Le "'Style paraît simple, mais il a une force merveilleuse': The *Mémoires et lettres de voyage* of Sophie de Hanovre. *Women in French Studies* 7 (special issue): 85–105.

Sophia of Hanover. 2013. *Memoirs (1630–1680)*. Edited and translated by Sean Ward. Toronto.

---

37. From Leibniz's notes on the manuscript, quoted by Van der Cruysse in Sophie de Hanovre 1990, 19.

Sophie de Hanovre. 1990. *Mémoires et Lettres de Voyage*. Edited by Dirk Van der
   Cruysse. Paris.
Strickland, Lloyd. 2011. *Leibniz and the Two Sophies: The Philosophical Corre-
   spondence*. Chicago.
Van der Cruysse, Dirk. 2005. *De Branche en Branche: Etudes sur le XVIIe et
   XVIIIe siècles français*. Louvain.
Van Horn, Jennifer. 2009. "The Mask of Civility: Portraits of Colonial Women
   and the Transatlantic Masquerade." *American Art* 23 (3): 8–35.
Velissariou, Aspasia. 2002. "'This thing was only designed for show and form':
   The Vicissitudes of Resemblance in Congreve's *Incognita*." *Journal of the
   Short Story in English* 39:23–40.

Chapter 4

"The Habit That Hides the Monk"

Missionary 'Masking' Strategies in Late Imperial Chinese Society and Court Culture*

Eugenio Menegon

ON 3 JUNE 1711, Matteo Ripa, a young Italian Catholic missionary and artist at the Chinese imperial court in Beijing, took up his pen to write a report to his superiors in Rome. Unlike most missionary-artists in China at the time, who were Jesuits, Ripa was an "apostolic missionary" of the papal Congregation for the Propagation of the Faith (Propaganda Fide). Ripa was no friend of the Jesuits. In his letter to Cardinal Giuseppe Sacripante, Prefect of Propaganda Fide in Rome, he reported details about his recent arrival in Beijing and his experience of inserting himself at court as a painter and printmaker. This was a common way for Catholic priests at the time to remain in China and try to obtain state patronage in the imperial capital for their confrères across the provinces of the empire. Ripa offered a scathing review of the lifestyle of the court Jesuits, criticizing them for their lavish Chinese-style clothes and comfortable life in these terms:

> They say that poverty cannot be practiced [here], but that a missionary who wants to come here has to dress richly, and similar arguments. They say that otherwise the [Chinese] will despise the missionaries and hold them in no esteem. To this I reply: "Are we here to be held in high esteem and to be honored by the Chinese?" ... In fact, my experience has been quite the opposite. In Canton I was dressed with cotton cloth, and no gentile among the many I met was scandalized. Actually, once they learned why [I was dressed in that manner], they felt edified.[1]

In his ascetic yearning, and very much in the Catholic tradition prizing the clerical habit, Ripa saw clothing as one of the central markers of religious life. "Dress-

---

* This chapter is an authorized reprint with minimal changes of Menegon 2020.
1. APF, SOCP Indie Orientali e Cina, vol. 26, fol. 313r.

ing richly" with silk gowns and owning multiple sets of robes for official purposes
and for use at home, as the Jesuits did in Beijing, seemed to him to completely
undermine the very essence of priestly and missionary vocation, and the vow of
poverty.

Yet his zeal was soon tempered by the intervention of his own superiors.
Even before he set foot at court, Ripa's spiritual director in Macao had com-
manded him to wear silk robes according to Chinese custom.[2] This was excessive
for Ripa's sense of religious poverty, so much so that he commented that "clothes
here are of so many kinds that they provoke much confusion."[3] He felt pressure
to conform, a pressure that came not just from the Jesuits but also from members
of the imperial court, and, most significantly, from the Bishop of Beijing and
Vicar Apostolic of Propaganda Fide, the Italian Reformed Franciscan Bernardino
della Chiesa. In 1715, four years after Ripa's arrival at court, Della Chiesa scolded
him for his stubborn sartorial resistance:

> I say to Your Lordship that in dressing you should comply
> with the others not only because of your singularity among
> so many Europeans, but also for the lack of respect that you
> show His Majesty and his courtiers, going to his presence
> and being with each other without the propriety [= *decenza*]
> in dressing required by the place and status. It would also
> be unusual in Europe if the prelates and domestics of His
> Holiness did not go dressed according to their statuses. The
> same would be the case in any court of European princes, if
> one of his courtiers were to dress as a plebeian. *We are here as*
> *if on a stage.* Your Lordship holds the position of courtier, and
> thus should comply with courtly dress.... It is my will that
> you dress in silk and comply with the others the best way you
> can.[4]

This conflict reveals in the clearest possible terms the importance of clothing
not only in religious life, where the use of the habit to proclaim an order's identity, as well as the social boundaries surrounding consecrated individuals, was
so prominent; it also demonstrates clothing's importance in society at large and
at the court in particular. Clothes were a tangible way to construct a hierarchy,
to mark distinctions, and to affirm social status, in early modern Europe and
late imperial China alike. Sumptuary laws prescribed what one could and could
not wear or consume, precisely to maintain social order, and rising classes of-

2. APF, SOCP Indie Orientali e Cina, vol. 26, fol. 313r.
3. APF, SOCP Indie Orientali e Cina, vol. 26, fol. 313r.
4. Van den Wyngaert and Mensaert 1954, vol. 5, 626. Italics mine.

ten challenged that order through their sartorial choices. China had a system of sumptuary laws and rituals that was even more intricate and stringent than those established across Europe, and it is not surprising that Ripa found the complexity of Chinese clothing bewildering.[5] By the late Ming, when missionaries arrived in China, a veritable "confusion of pleasure" had scrambled the clothing hierarchy, and urban rich merchants in particular challenged dress and consumption legal restrictions at every turn.[6]

For the Jesuits the matter was complicated by their religious status, which required yet another set of clerical dress rules. Reports and letters, lists of accounts, inventories, and similar materials reveal that clothing was one of the first concerns that missionaries encountered in China, and it was not a trivial one. Clothing and bodily practices can be viewed as a gauge of broader issues in the history of the encounter between China and the West, and in the history of Jesuit and Christian presence there, and demonstrate how "going local" was an inevitable outcome in China.

THE JESUITS AND THEIR APPROACH TO CLOTHING: THE FOUNDATIONAL YEARS IN EUROPE

Over a century before Ripa had to face his sartorial choices in Beijing, the first Jesuit missionaries arrived in China on Portuguese ships. Europeans in East Asia had to play by the rules of native powers, and that included the adoption of local diplomatic ceremonial, and respect for the social and cultural order of those countries.

By the time the Jesuits were founded in the mid-sixteenth century, ecclesiastical clothing had already accumulated over a millennium of historical development, from the simple tunics of the first monks in the Middle Eastern deserts, to the variety of male and female habits of the medieval and early modern monastic and mendicant orders.[7] The Protestant Reformation, however, provoked a deep reflection on religious life within Catholicism, and one of the consequences was the emergence of a new category of religious men, the "clerics regular."[8] The Jesuits belonged to this new wave of priests, who followed rules adapted to more intense social interactions, entailing freedom of movement and inconspicuous appearance for the purpose of apostolic work. Their habit had to be functional for works of charity, education, and religious duties among the laity, and while clearly inspired by "ecclesiastical dress," it had no strict requirements. Like other clerics regular, Jesuits dressed in a generic cassock, which simply imitated that

5. "Sumptuary Laws and Changing Styles," in Wilkinson 2022, 119–22.
6. Brook 1998, 130–36.
7. Rocca 2000.
8. Rocca 2000, 103.

of "reputable priests," as mentioned in the founding Formulas of the Society of Jesus.[9] The Latin word used there for "reputable" was *honestus*, a word that appears again in the original Spanish text of the Jesuit Constitutions drafted by Ignatius of Loyola and his early Jesuit companions.[10] The habit had to be locally "accommodated" to the place where one lived, following church tradition. Last, the habit had to be modest and inexpensive, in compliance with the vow of poverty. Generally speaking, the vagueness of Loyola's prescriptions encouraged some variety in clothing in the early history of the Society, and even produced some controversy.[11]

Even after uniformity was reached, the habit continued to remain a signifier of internal hierarchy between the priests and the lay brothers ("temporal coadjutors"). The brothers were Jesuits as well, but received limited education, so that they would remain humble and within their professional niche as manual laborers.[12] Their difference in rank also took visual form in their clothing, with their cassocks and cloaks shorter than those of the priests. They were also encouraged to wear a round hat instead of the square biretta, a symbol of the priestly educational and spiritual position. The brothers, however, fought for almost a century to maintain the use of the biretta, resorting to petitioning more than one pope, and finally losing that privilege in 1645. These apparently cosmetic sartorial choices had, in fact, important consequences, and some brothers lost their vocation and left the Society after feeling humiliated by the changes.[13]

This situation seems to reveal a contradiction: on the one hand, clothing was "indifferent" and adaptable. On the other hand, however, it also was increasingly uniform, subtly hierarchical, and thus laden with power and meaning. The habit had to conceal the shape of the body, conferring a second protective skin, even a halo of supernatural aloofness, while avoiding any sexual innuendo. It also represented poverty and penance, and thus often had the shape of sackcloth. Yet its main function was to distinguish the priests and nuns from the laity, and to affirm an established societal and spiritual order.

MISSIONARY CLOTHES AND BODILY PRACTICES IN MING CHINA

European expansion in the sixteenth century confronted the church with non-Christian societies and their customs and clothing across the globe, includ-

---

9. Padberg 1996, 12; for a general discussion of clothing and identity among the early Jesuits, see Levy 2011.

10. Spanish original in Loyola's *Constitutiones*, Codina 1936, vol. 2, 543; English version in Padberg 1996, 12; compare "Kleidung," in Koch 1962, 986–88.

11. On the discussions surrounding Jesuit clothing in Spain in the 1560s, see Borràs 1967.

12. Ganss 1981, 35.

13. "Bonete de los Hermanos Coadiutores," in Astrain 1916, 289–90.

ing in East Asia.[14] After their arrival in Japan in the late 1540s, the Jesuits wore the silk robes of the Buddhist monks, to earn the same kind of respect they enjoyed in local society.[15] Following some soul searching and controversy within the Japan mission, the famous Jesuit visitor Alessandro Valignano then initiated the policy of accommodation that was also applied in China in the 1580s, when Michele Ruggieri and Matteo Ricci started their efforts to settle within the Ming empire.[16] At first, local officials in Guangdong province asked Ruggieri to adopt the identity and the clothes of Buddhist monks.[17] Valignano swiftly approved the move. This entailed shaving any facial hair, wearing very short hair, and donning Buddhist robes. Ricci characterized this attire, adopted by the Fathers and all their servants between 1582 and 1595, as *"honesta"* – the same word used by Loyola – specifying that the robe was "modest and long, with long sleeves, not very different from our [Jesuit robe]."[18] At the suggestion of the Chinese literatus Qu Taisu 瞿太素, Ricci and his companions started shedding the identity of Buddhist monks, considered a disreputable group by many in the Confucian elite. Soon Valignano approved the use of "proper silk garments for visiting magistrates and other important persons who, on visits, wear ceremonial dress and hats."[19] Ricci and his companion Lazzaro Cattaneo grew long beards and hair in the second half of 1594, and in May 1595 Ricci paid a visit to an official dressed for the first time as a Chinese scholar.[20] Ricci described his new wardrobe as including at least two silk gowns, one for public visits, and the other to wear at home.[21] The earliest known oil portrait of Ricci, still kept in Rome, only gives us an idea of the robe worn at home.[22] The one used for visits, sketched in an early xylograph of Ricci, was far richer and not for practical use, and was known as a "ceremonial robe" or *lifu* (禮服) (see Figure 1). Actually, Ricci's robe differed from those authorized by Ming sumptuary laws for degree-holders and officials, as he said himself: "Those who have neither office nor grade but are persons of importance also have appropriate visiting-dress, different from that of the ordi-

14. For a global treatment of missionary clothing, see, e.g., Sanfilippo 1996, 1997, 2000.

15. Valignano 2011, 152–53; compare Schütte 1980–85, vol. 2, 245.

16. Hoey 2010; Zampol D'Ortia 2016. A visitor in the Jesuit order was a commissar with wide powers to inspect communities and recommend policy changes.

17. Ruggieri to Acquaviva, Zhaoqing, 7 February 1583, in OS, vol. 2, 416.

18. FR, vol. 1, 192. On Jesuit clothing in this phase, see also Bettray 1955, 4–10; Peterson 1994; Hsia 2010, 138.

19. FR, vol. 1, 337; compare Harris 1966, 89.

20. OS, vol. 2, 136.

21. OS, vol. 2, 199; translated in Harris 1966, 90.

22. On 24 August 1617, Girolamo Alaleoni SJ so described the famous portrait at the Professed House of the College of the Gesù in Rome: "The portrait of our Fr. Matteo has been hanging for several weeks in the entrance hall of this house with those of our other Blessed Jesuits. But the image does not depict the Father as he would go outside … but rather *as he dresses at home, without fan and solemn dress*" (italics mine); see OS, vol. 2, 497. On this portrait see also Guillen-Nuñez 2014.

Figure 1. Portrait of Matteo Ricci in Life of Master Li Xitai from
the Great West (Daxi Xitai Li xiansheng xingji 大西西泰利先生行
蹟). Manuscript copy made in 1636 [original printed edition 1630].
Courtesy of the Bibliothèque nationale de France, Paris, Chinois
996.

nary people, and which we have adopted in this kingdom."[23] From then on, this became the accepted wardrobe for Jesuits in Ming China.

One of the great masters of European painting, Rubens, drew an almost photographic reproduction of a Jesuit *lifu*. That famous image portrays the procurator of the China mission Nicolas Trigault, who returned from China with important business in 1616–17.[24] One remarkable feature in the new garb was the hat, which in the early portraits of Ricci appears, as he put it, "somewhat like a bishop's miter."[25] This was called a "Dongpo hat," from the name of the famous Song-dynasty poet and scholar Su Shi 蘇軾, also known as Su Dongpo 蘇東坡, who allegedly popularized it. In the late Ming, this hat, prized for its association with antiquity, was worn by literati who had not attained an official degree, by those who were no longer in an official position, or by officials who did not wear their insignia of rank in private life.[26] Trigault's portrait, however, reproduced a different kind of hat, as did the portrait of another procurator to Europe, Álvaro Semedo, thirty years later (see Figure 2). This was a "square hat" (fangjin 方巾) worn by students and literati without a degree but also by officials of lower rank whenever they were not wearing insignia.

Last, the China Jesuits followed a new bodily practice, adopting a long beard and growing their hair long, as was the norm in Ming China. Their hair was collected in a knot and hidden under a hat. Long beards, however, were difficult to grow for most Chinese, and they were usually an attribute of old age that symbolized wisdom. Ricci observed that "the men have sparse beards or none at all; what little facial hair they have is completely straight and it is so late in growing that a man of thirty might be taken among us for twenty."[27] He also mentioned that men, except for children and Buddhist monks, would let their hair and beards grow without ever shaving during their lifetime. The decision of the missionaries to adopt the persona of the literatus and to abandon that of the Buddhist monk by growing their beards to the longest possible length, was made together with Valignano. Ricci wrote in 1595 that he let his facial hair grow "because in China a long beard is a rare thing (è cosa rara)"[28] A seventeenth-century source described Ricci's physical appearance in this way: "A curly beard, green eyes, and a voice like a great bell."[29] The curly, long beard was obviously one of the physical traits that stood out in Chinese eyes. Long hair and beards signaled age, and age in China

23. Harris 1966, 90.
24. Logan and Brockey 2003, 157; compare also Alsteens 2014.
25. OS, vol. 2, 199; translated in Harris 1966, 90.
26. Cortes 2001, 374; Ricci calls the hat *sutumpo*, see FR, vol. 1, 358.
27. FR, vol. I, 88; compare also OS, vol. 2, 157.
28. OS, vol. 2, 173.
29. *Kangxi Renhe xianzhi, juan* 22, 22–23.

P. Aluaro Semedo Portughese, della Comp.ª di Giesu, Venuto a Roma
Procurator delle Prou.ᵉ del Giapone et della China, nell'an. 1642.

Figure 2. Álvaro Semedo's portrait, published in his Historica relatione del Gran Regno della Cina (Rome 1653). Public domain, CC BY-SA 4.0.

meant authority and gravitas. Another possible reason for the Jesuits' adoption of long beards was that they were attempting to put a greater distance between themselves and women, who had contacts with priests for confession, holy mass, and other sacraments. The mature and distinguished looks of long-bearded and robed Jesuits, together with the presence of male chaperons from the women's families, made such encounters even more detached, establishing a clear gender demarcation.[30]

The apparently uncontroversial adoption of the literati robes during Ricci's lifetime, with the blessing of visitor Valignano, however, did not completely silence criticism on the use of silk, both within the Society and from other missionary orders, as it was considered a breach of the poverty vow and was a decision that directly contravened the Constitutions and Loyola's opinion. During the late 1620s, another Jesuit visitor, André Palmeiro (1569–1635), had to face some tensions over the use of the silk robe between the members of the Japanese Province, by then mostly exiled to Macao after the prohibition of Christianity in visitation to the General in Rome, he regarded this matter as one of the most important reasons for the inspection, dedicating a separate report to clothing alone.[31]

Palmeiro also made an important statement on the meaning of the religious habit, and its relationship to the special identity of the Jesuits as a new order of men working in the world:

> There is no doubt that it is not yet the time nor the timely conjunction for our men residing within China *to wear a particular habit or an identifiable mark on their external attire by which to be recognized by all as a specific family or congregation. We must all be one, but without being known as such.* Nor should we declare this fact to the simple folks, but we do explain it to those who are more intelligent, who understand it perfectly.[32]

Here the visitor formulated the Jesuit strategic intention of maintaining a hidden identity and using the garments of the Chinese literati to blend into society, while masking – at least to the non-initiated – their true religious identity. After consultation with veterans of the mission, however, the visitor also ordered members of the Chinese vice-province to discontinue the use of silk gowns for daily use, as he had noted excesses. For example, Trigault alone owned five sets of personal silk garments. In more established Christian communities, the abolition of silk robes in daily use was a feasible expectation, as Chinese elites had become familiar with

30. Menegon 2006, 39–40; Menegon 2009, 230–36; Amsler 2018, 26–27.
31. Brockey 2014, 302–306.
32. Brockey 2014, 303; original Portuguese in ARSI, JS 161-II, fol. 114r. Italics mine.

the Jesuits' emphasis on the austerity of religious life, and would understand their modesty, especially if some members of the local gentry had converted. However, Palmeiro also gave special powers to the vice-provincial to grant exemptions and still allow silk for courtesy robes to meet officials. Given this latitude, there were still silken domestic robes depicted in portraits, such as that of Semedo in 1642.

More research is needed to clarify what truly happened beyond prescriptive regulations. The 1630s and 1640s were times of great upheaval in China. The Ming dynasty had plunged into a great internal crisis, beset by famine, peasant rebellions, and military collapse, while the rising power of the Manchus in the north represented a challenge that would eventually engulf the empire and lead to dynastic change. Starting in the 1630s, the number of high members of the elites interested in Jesuit teachings in matters of science as well as morality and religion dramatically decreased, while the solidity of grassroots Christian communities increased. The need for contacts with elites and especially with officials to obtain patronage diminished as well.

The growth of native Christian communities allowed for the dispensing of personal silk gowns but also for the acceptance of sumptuous liturgical vestments for communitarian worship. A late Ming Chinese text on the mass by the Italian Jesuit Giulio Aleni (1582–1649) explains that the garments must be magnificent in order to offer sacrifice to God. The most peculiar vestment he described was a special hat invented for the celebration of the mass in China, called a "sacrificial hat" (jijin 祭巾) (see Figure 3).[33] This bonnet became necessary because, unlike in Europe, in China meeting a superior with a bare head was considered extremely disrespectful.

Missionary Clothes and Bodily Practices in Qing China

The Ming-Qing transition was an immensely traumatic event. Untold numbers of people died in fighting, famines, and sieges between the mid-1640s and the 1650s. Many men committed suicide to avoid serving the Manchu invaders, who were the founders of the new Qing dynasty, and many women did the same to avoid rape and family disgrace. One of the new Manchu laws that traumatized Ming men like no other was the infamous order to cut their hair according to Manchu fashion, and to change their style of clothing. This shows how central hairstyles and clothing were to Ming Chinese masculinity.[34] The explosive issue

33. On the *jijin*, see Anonymous 1924, 376–77, 404–6; Dudink 2007, 219; Philippi Collection Online (private collection of religious hats, Kirkel, Saarland, Germany) http://philippi-collection. blogspot.com/2011/07/chinese-jijin-tsikin-tsikim-tsi-kim.html. The Chinese text on the *jijin* is in Giulio Aleni's *Misa jiyi* 彌撒祭義 (The meaning of the sacrifice of the mass), *juan* 1, fol. 15a6–15b7, reprinted in CCT BNF, vol. 16, 513–14, compare Bontinck 1962, 58, note 122; for the 1615 request to Rome of permission to celebrate the Mass with the head covered, see ibid., 36–37, 40–41.

34. Wilkinson 2022, 327–29; Spence et al. 2013, "Two edicts," 26–28.

Figure 3. Portrait of Giulio Aleni wearing the *jijin*, from *Life of Master Ai Siji from the Great West* (*Taixi Siji Ai xiansheng xingshu* 泰西思及艾先生行述). Manuscript copy made in 1689 [originally composed ca. 1650]. Courtesy of the Bibliothèque nationale de France, Paris, Chinois 1017.

of men's hair led to rebellions in 1645 in the lower Yangzi regions. The Chinese believed that the crown of the head was medically sensitive, that it was unfilial to shave one's hair, and that doing so signaled a renunciation of sexuality. Most significantly, the new hairdo represented submission to the barbarians.[35]

The Jesuits, who had chosen to be seen as members of the literati elite, rather than as Buddhist or Daoist clergy – the only subjects exempted from the hair cutting decrees – had no choice but to follow the Manchu directives. They also did so because their loyalty was not to a specific dynasty – or even to an ethnic or cultural order – but rather to a timeless divine plan for the conversion of the Chinese empire. Most missionaries became instant turncoats once the triumphant Manchu troops reached their locales.

The new Manchu rulers immediately coopted the Jesuits for their technical knowledge, and after occupying Beijing in 1644 they named the Jesuit Adam Schall von Bell as co-director of the Imperial Astronomical Directorate, a post that Catholic missionaries kept almost without interruption until 1838. Schall did not describe in detail his adoption of the Manchu hairstyle or clothing at the time of the Manchu entry into the capital. He only mentioned that when he surrendered wearing *commoner's clothes* (probably still in Ming style), he petitioned the Manchu authorities on his knees to allow him to remain in his residence in the "Tartar City" – thus avoiding forced eviction with the Han population, all transferred outside the walls into the new and makeshift "Chinese City." In his later reports, Schall mentioned that, once he received a bureaucratic appointment, he agreed to wear Qing official robes with insignia corresponding to his rank (see Figure 4).[36]

The surrender of Schall's confrère Martino Martini in southern China is described in much greater detail. During the summer of 1646 in Yanping, Fujian, Martini first accepted the orders of the southern Ming Longwu Emperor to wear Ming official robes, after apparently turning down a position offered to him to facilitate a military alliance with the Portuguese in Macao against the Manchus. Within four months, however, Martini submitted to the triumphant Qing troops in the region of Wenzhou, in southern Zhejiang province.[37] In his bestseller *De bello Tartarico* (On the Tartar War, Antwerp, 1654), Martini described his shift in dynastic loyalty in the presence of a Manchu military commander. The highly symbolic act of surrender and declaration of allegiance pivoted around the shaving of his hair and the shifting of his clothes to the new style:

35. Wilkinson 2022, 327–29.
36. Schall 1942, 157.
37. On the murky circumstances of Martini's whereabouts just before his surrender and his shifting loyalties, see Menegon 1998. A description of the Ming robe bestowed on Martini in Biermann 1955, 223; a 1654 portrait of Martini in Qing attire by Michaelina Woutiers is discussed in Golvers 2016.

Figure 4. Adam Schall in Qing official robe, from Athanasius Kircher, *China monumentis illustrata* (Amsterdam 1670). Courtesy of the Universitätsbibliothek Bern.

> The Tartar commander ... asked me if I was ready to change
> by my own accord *my hair style and Chinese clothes*. I agreed,
> and he ordered me to shave my hair in his presence. I then
> gestured to him that that kind of shaven head did not fit with
> Chinese clothes any longer, and he took off his leggings, gave
> them to me to wear, and put his Tartar hat on my head.[38]

Martini commended the new Manchu hat as "a comfortable and elegant orna-ment," and this positive reaction contrasted with his assessment of the care shown by Ming men for their long hair, in a language that implied a condemnation of the practice, which he probably deemed unmanly.[39] He added elsewhere a com-mentary on the beauty, straightforwardness, and human touch of the Manchus, which left no doubt as to his preference for them over the "effete" Han Chinese.[40] He ridiculed the Chinese for putting up a mighty resistance to the hair-cutting edict, "preoccupied more with their own hair than their own native land."[41]

Under Manchu rule the diatribes on the use of silk continued to simmer, es-pecially because members of the newly arrived Dominican and Franciscan orders started to criticize the ways of the Jesuits.[42] Martini, therefore, while in Rome as procurator in 1655, wrote a memorial to the General, mentioning the need for the China Jesuits to wear common (*suté*, that is, *sude*, simple 素的) kinds of silk, reiterating as well that silk was not a particularly prestigious fabric in China, and that even farmers used it.[43] By this time, it appears, the Jesuits had developed a protocol that simply followed a general principle of adapting to the clothing of the literati, whatever the style was in accordance with dynastic sumptuary laws and current practices. New regime, new clothes: no big deal.

MISSIONARIES AT THE QING COURT

The Jesuits had no qualms about adopting the new attire and wearing official Qing robes when some of them attained positions within the Chinese bureau-cracy. Once the German astronomer Adam Schall became an official, and for some time a favorite of the young Shunzhi Emperor, he wore sumptuous of-ficial robes in the new style, including Qing official hats with rank buttons. In his 1661 apologetic *Historica Relatio*, Schall mentions how he tried to turn down bureaucratic posts, but finally had to give in and wear Qing official robes

38. Martini, 2013, vol. 5, 280 (Martini 1654, 100).
39. Martini, 2013, vol. 5, 226–27 (Martini 1654, 38–39).
40. Martini, 2013, vol. 5, 227 (Martini 1654, 40).
41. Martini, 2013, vol. 5, 275 (Martini 1654, 95).
42. Biermann 1955; Menegon, 1998.
43. Martini 1998, vol. 1, 309.

with insignia corresponding to his rank, obeying orders from Vice-Provincial Francisco Furtado.[44]

Schall soon became a controversial figure not only for his work in astronomy, which some in the church considered tainted by Chinese calendrical superstition, but also because of his extravagant lifestyle and arrogant behavior toward other Jesuits. His confrère in Beijing Gabriel de Magalhães started a veritable war against him, writing long reports to the visitor of China and Japan, Manuel de Azevedo, in 1649, denouncing Schall's great expenses for an excessive number of personal fine clothes and hats, as well as for official robes decorated with dragons.[45] His best-known portrait in official garb shows the sumptuousness of his attire; the robe sports an embroidered "mandarin square" on his chest with a white crane, symbol of the first rank (see Figure 4).[46] The complaints against Schall required the creation of two special disciplinary commissions in Rome in the 1660s to decide whether he was guilty of superstitious practice and excessive extravagance. He was finally exonerated because of the great advantages of his position for the church and the mission in China and the possible dangers had he refused his official position.[47] The early internal arguments among Jesuits on clothing, silk, and poverty in China increasingly became the weapons of enemies outside the Society of Jesus – Dominicans, Franciscans, Foreign Missions of Paris – to attack them for breaking the rules of religious life, especially at court.

Over the course of the late seventeenth and eighteenth centuries the wardrobe for attending ceremonies at the palace or work in the imperial workshops became codified in sumptuary laws following court etiquette. After the attacks on Schall's extravagance and his high rank at court, his successor at the Directorate of Astronomy, Ferdinand Verbiest, also had to face opposition within the Society of Jesus concerning his acceptance of high office in the Qing administration.[48] In 1681, he defended the Jesuit policy of wearing Chinese silk robes according to the current literati fashion from the attacks of the Dominican Domingo Fernandez Navarrete, simply noting that all successors of Ricci followed his wise policy of sartorial adaptation, avoiding splendor, and showing religious gravity in their dress.[49]

44. Schall 1942, 157.

45. Passages from Magalhães, "Apontamentos do modo de viver e proceder do Padre João Adão nesta Corte …," Letter to the Visitor and Vice-Provincial of China, 1649 ? (ARSI, JS 142, no. 32, fol. 3r), edited in Pih 1979, 256, 328, 330.

46. Schall's color portrait was originally painted by his confrère Johannes Grueber in 1659–1660 in Beijing: see Pih 1979, 362; Väth 1991, 238, 351–352; Chang 1998. On the insignia of rank, see Cammann 1944.

47. Pih 1979; Romano 2016.

48. On the diatribes against Verbiest within the Society of Jesus, see Malatesta and Rouleau 1994, 485–94; on his Qing ranks and his attempts to turn them down but also his politicking to obtain the position of Director, see Vande Walle 1994, 501.

49. Verbiest 1938, 307; Golvers 2017, 362.

While the missionaries' daily wardrobe in the provinces also became stan-
dardized according to the new Qing fashion and was gradually accepted by all
orders, requirements for those working at the palace were much more stringent.[50]
Only very few missionaries who occupied official posts in the Astronomical Directorate wore special robes with embroidered chest squares according to their
ranking, and only when called for ceremonial audiences at the palace. Their normal "work" attire was that of well-dressed elites. By the eighteenth century, a
consensus had been reached and controversies over the use of silk were no longer
center-stage, but formal silk robes had become part and parcel of the identity of
any China missionary, especially for those serving at the court.

However, due to the extreme continental climate of the capital, swinging
from torrid summers to freezing and windy winters, the wardrobe had to be
varied according to the season. Ripa observed that in Beijing in winter even com-
moners wore,

> over a long cotton shirt, a jacket padded with lambskin or
> other fur. On top, they wear an external shirt padded with
> cotton, long to the knees, and over that, the *paozi* (袍子),
> that is, a robe reaching the feet, lined with fox or ermine.
> Over the *paozi*, they wear a *waitao* (外套), a kind of short
> tunic, also lined with fox or ermine. Moreover, when it snows
> they wear a mantel, long almost all the way to the ground,
> lined on the outside with otter skins (*cane marino*).[51]

In summer it was necessary to wear light garments: a refreshing shirt made of
kudzu vine fiber (gepu 葛布), covered by a *paozi* of the same light fabric, and
on top a *waitao* made of *sha* (沙) silk gauze. Ripa added that a great variety of
other garments were necessary for the mid-seasons as well; these garments were
increasingly lighter when nearing summer, and, inversely, heavier when progress-
ing toward winter. Almost exasperated by this complexity, he concluded: "This
is something that is not practiced anywhere in any other part of the world, no
matter how cultivated and delicate such place might be."[52]

All these garments cost dearly. Teodorico Pedrini commented in 1742 about
the high expenses for clothes to attend functions or simply work at the imperial
palaces, especially since they had to be varied according to seasons and type of
ceremony, "now of one kind of fur, now of another; now of a certain color, now

50. Lucas Tomás, circular letter to the Fathers of the Seraphic Mission, Canton, 21 January
1705, in Margiotti 1975, vol. 8, 779–80.
51. Ripa 1996, vol. 2, 4–5.
52. Ripa 1996, vol. 2, 4–5.

of another." On one occasion, he even borrowed a robe from the Chief Eunuch, as his own *waitao* was black, a color forbidden at court that day.[53] The Discalced Augustinian Sigismondo Meinardi da San Nicola, a court clockmaker, in 1752 confirmed the high expense needed to appear at the palace, "where one has to be neatly dressed from head to toe. I spent in one year for such clothing more than in the twelve years I lived in Beijing before being called to the palace."[54] Elsewhere he added that he had to spend much in "proper, albeit ordinary, clothes, which have always to be according to propriety as we see the emperor every day."[55] His confrère Anselmo da Santa Margherita confirmed in 1793 that the Beijing missionaries needed a multi-seasonal "honest" wardrobe (vestire onestamente), especially because of their courtly roles. Even those who had no technical functions at the palace, in fact had to participate in ceremonies of greetings to the emperor four times a year: on the Chinese New Year; at the return of the emperor from the Yuanmingyuan suburban villa after winter; at his departure for the hunting resort of Chengde in the spring; and at his return from the hunts in the fall.[56] Church authorities in Rome suggested that "that both in their clothing and their general outside appearance [missionaries] show a certain dignity and decency," to make clear to their Chinese audience that they were serving the court not out of any economic need or personal greed, but only to support their religion.[57] While the Jesuits spent generously on their attire, the meager subsidies of Propaganda could often reduce their men to a look that conjured "not religious poverty, but rather vile sordidness."[58]

The imperial bestowal of silk bolts as payment for services, and the occasional free tailoring of robes and fur coats under imperial order for the missionaries, underlined the central preoccupation with clothing in courtly life in Beijing and how the gifting of clothes was considered a common form of compensation for court missionaries. In 1738, the Discalced Augustinian miniature painter Serafino da San Giovanni Battista, for example, reported that upon his and Meinardi's arrival in the capital from Europe, the emperor had ordered that they "measure

53. Pedrini to Procurator Miralta, Beijing, 2 November 1742 (APF, Procura Cina, Box 1, fol. 1v).

54. Meinardi to Procurator Guglielmi, Beijing, 10 September 1752 (APF, Procura Cina, Box 15, fol. 1r).

55. Sigismondo Meinardi to Prefect of Propaganda, 30 November 1752 (APF, SOCP Indie Orientali e Cina, vol. 50, fol. 207v).

56. Anselmo da Santa Margherita to Prefect of Propaganda, Beijing, 25 October 1793 (APF, SOCP Indie Orientali e Cina, vol. 68, fol. 647r–653r).

57. Ex-Jesuits Ventavon and Poirot to Propaganda, 1779 (APF, Acta CP Indie Orientali e Cina, vol. 14, fol. 45v).

58. Ex-Jesuits Ventavon and Poirot to Propaganda, 1779 (APF, Acta CP Indie Orientali e Cina, vol. 14, fol. 45v).

our sizes for a *waitao* and a *paozi*, one to be lined with ermine, and the other with sable" and that "the lining was of high quality, and the cloth on top quite beautiful."[59] Practices changed with time, possibly also linked to the declining imperial favor toward the missionaries. In 1764, for example, the court artisan and Discalced Carmelite Arcangelo Maria di Sant'Anna observed that in the past the emperor had generously ordered the court tailors to take the Europeans' measurements during the summer months and prepare a complete fur coat for the coming winter. That practice, however, had more recently been abandoned in favor of the cheaper bestowal of bolts of ordinary silk "barely sufficient to clothe us for a few years, [and, moreover, for robes to be worn] only at home."[60] During the latter part of the eighteenth century, especially after the dissolution of the Society of Jesus in China in 1775, the Beijing mission entered into a long phase of decline, and the number of court missionaries dwindled. The last lone survivor, the Portuguese Lazarist Cayetano Pires Pereira, Apostolic Administrator of Beijing, died on the eve of the Opium Wars in 1838. He was still formally charged with the position of Co-Director of the Astronomical Directorate and thus wore and was portrayed with official robes.

CONCLUSION: ACCOMMODATION, DISSIMULATION, OR NECESSITY?

On his way back to his Beijing mission, the French Jesuit Jean de Fontaney wrote from London in 1704 to a Jesuit correspondent in France on the matter of silk clothing. Referring to his recent tour of France as procurator of the China French Jesuit mission, he reported the criticism of someone who had asked him:

> You go around dressed in silk in China and you do not walk
> about the cities, but you use sedan chairs. Did the apostles
> preach the Gospel in this manner? And how can one respect
> religious poverty while dressing with silken gowns?

He replied:

> Our China missionaries are the brothers of those who go
> barefoot with penitential clothes and who fast austerely in
> the missions of Madurai [in India]; and of those who follow
> in the snow the savages of the forests of Canada, suffering
> cold and hunger.... Is it a relaxation of rules that the Jesuits
> in Canada can eat meat, while those in India never eat it? ...
> *What is good and sufficient in one country to have the Gospel*

59. Serafino da San Giovanni Battista to Procurator Miralta, Beijing, 11 May 1738 (APF, Procura Cina, Box 30, fol. 3r).

60. Arcangelo Maria di Santa Anna to Procurator Palladini, Haidian, 30 September 1764 (APF, Procura Cina, Box 14, fol. 1r).

accepted, in some cases does not work at all or is insufficient in another country.[61]

This was the ultimate rationale for proclaiming the Ignatian "indifference" to material accidents in the pursuit of souls and for defending the importance of a "habit that hid the monk," allowing the missionaries to move stealthily in Chinese society, both in the provinces – especially after 1724 when they all became clandestine following the imperial prohibition of Christian proselytization – and in the capital, where they continued to occupy official and technical positions to protect the illegal activities of their confrères across the empire. The words by de Fontaney reflect a clear Jesuit strategy surrounding clothing and the body. As long as the aim of conversion and the religious message were kept central, the means remained indifferent. There were, however, limits on the adoption of extravagant or luxurious attires, and restraints had to be put in place to avoid the corrosion of ethical standards and religious discipline, which in turn would endanger the entire edifice of the mission.

Scholars have used various intellectual frameworks to understand missionary adaptability. Many have espoused the concept of accommodation, also called the *modo suave* (soft method), especially in non-European contexts. The word *"accomodare"* (to accommodate) is often found in primary sources in relation to missions.[62] Others have explored the culture of "dissimulation" so typical of the Baroque era, an age of religious conflicts and rhetorical masking, as a possible source of Jesuit flexibility. Contemporary critics, both Catholic and Protestant, actually accused the Jesuits of duplicity, travesty, and simulation, including in their Asian missions.[63]

Communication of Catholic and European ideas and practices occurred at different levels in China: through the "apostolate of the book" written in Chinese; through scientific propaganda; through the proxy of native catechists and their oral ministry; through priestly rituality enacted in the liturgy and the sacraments; and through the materiality of objects (pictures, amulets, luxury items for the court, etc.) that mediated concepts, channeled spiritual forces, and facilitated relationships. Clothes were yet another powerful way to communicate. In this case, Chinese-style apparel communicated to the Chinese public and the imperial court that the missionaries had been readily assimilated to the native culture of China, and that the alterity of the "Western Ocean men" (*Xiyang ren* 西洋人), as Europeans were called, had been neutralized and domesticated, in the time-honored Confucian process of *jiaohua* 教化, that is, "transformation through teaching" of Chinese ethics, language, literature, and customs.

Here I have approached the topic of clothing and bodily practices from the

61. LEC, vol. 3, 136 and 138. Italics mine.
62. Muller 2016.
63. See, e.g., Hsia 2002; Levy 2011; Pavone 2013.

classic point of view of accommodation, and the European missionaries themselves have been the actors at the center of the historical stage, literally clothed
in Chinese costumes. The Chinese evolving material circumstances in the Ming-
Qing period, however, powerfully influenced missionary accommodation from
the outside. Dressing like the natives was absolutely necessary for the survival of
the missionary enterprise. It allowed the foreign missioners to be inconspicuous
and to become culturally acceptable, even before becoming culturally proficient.
This was doubly important at the court, as missionaries were closely observed
"as if on a stage" by the imperial family and the metropolitan bureaucracy. They
needed to show respect for courtly etiquette and sumptuary laws, and visibly fit
within the hierarchies of power; this included using their bodies and attire. Wearing European clothes was thus never a possibility. Selecting the best social image
that certain local clothes conveyed – the attire of the literati elite rather than
that of the Buddhist or Daoist clergy – was, to an extent, a choice. That choice,
nevertheless, was not made independently but rather at the suggestion of Chinese
interlocutors, both literati and officials. Indeed, a new path away from Buddhist
clerical identity emerged only after native informants offered their crucial input,
a fact that confirms how the actions of missionaries in China were shaped by the
Chinese social and material context, as much as they were by the missionaries'
own spiritual tradition and modus operandi.[64] Li Zhizao 李之藻, one of the
most prominent literati converts of the late Ming period, put it quite clearly:

> After Ricci entered China, for several years he followed a con-
> fused path (*hunji* 混跡). Then he met Qu Taisu, who deemed
> that it was not appropriate to behave like a Buddhist monk.
> Following this, Ricci let his hair grow and started identifying
> himself as a Confucian who had come to China to admire its
> superior civilization.[65]

In this Chinese rendering of the story, Ricci hardly seems to have been the one
in charge.

The tension within the missionary community between the uniformity of
religious rules and attire, on the one hand, and the need to adapt to a diversity
of places and cultures, on the other, never completely disappeared, but certainly
became attenuated over time. Our scholarly interpretation of how this tension
played out depends on how we read the sources and what perspective, Chinese or
missionary, we privilege in our reading of those sources. In this chapter we have
mainly heard the words of the missionaries themselves, grappling with the reper-
cussions of their "going local." Yet, the voices of their Chinese counterparts – the

---

64. Standaert 1999.
65. FR, vol. 1, 336, note 1; Chinese original text in Li 1965, *juan* 1, 13a.

Confucian literati, the provincial and court officials, the eunuchs, the emperor, and the common men and women of the Ming and Qing empires – were never so far in the background as to become inaudible.

BIBLIOGRAPHY

Abbreviations

Acta CP	*Acta della Congregazione particolare dell'Indie Orientali e Cina*
APF	Archivio Storico della Congregazione per l'Evangelizzazione dei Popoli o "de Propaganda Fide," Rome
ARSI	Archivum Romanum Societatis Iesu, Rome
CCT BnF	Standaert, et al. *Faguo guojia tushuguan Ming-Qing Tianzhujiao wenxian* 法國國家圖書館明清天主教文獻 (Chinese Christian texts from the National Library of France)
FR	D'Elia, *Fonti Ricciane*
LEC	Aimé-Martin, *Lettres édifiantes et curieuses*
OS	Tacchi-Venturi, *Opere Storiche del P. Matteo Ricci*
SOCP	*Scritture originali della Congregazione particolare dell'Indie Orientali e Cina*

Online publications

Philippi, Dieter. Philippi Collection Online (private collection of religious hats, Kirkel, Saarland, Germany) https://philippi-collection.de/en/

Archival Sources

Archivio Storico della Congregazione per l'Evangelizzazione dei Popoli o "de Propaganda Fide" (APF), Rome
Acta CP [Acta della Congregazione particolare dell'Indie Orientali e Cina]
SOCP [Scritture originali della Congregazione particolare dell'Indie Orientali e Cina]
Procura Cina
Archivum Romanum Societatis Iesu (ARSI), Rome
Japonica Sinica
Fondo Gesuitico

Printed Primary Sources

Aleni, Giulio. 2010 [or. ed. 1630]. *Vita del maestro Ricci, Xitai del Grande Occidente (Daxi Xitai Li xiansheng xingji,* 大西西泰利先生行蹟), Chinese text and Italian translation by Gianni Criveller. Brescia.

Aimé-Martin, M. Louis, ed. **[LEC]**. 1843. *Lettres édifiantes et curieuses concernant l'Asie, l'Afrique et l'Amérique, avec quelques relations nouvelles des missions, et des notes géographiques et historiques.* Pantheon litteraire, vol. 3. Paris.

[Codina, Arturo, ed.]. 1936. *Monumenta Ignatiana: ex autographis vel ex antiquioribus exemplis collecta: series tertia, Sancti Ignatii de Loyola Constitutiones Societatis Jesu. Tomo 2. Textus hispanus.* Monumenta historica Societatis Iesu, vol. 64. Rome.

Cortes, Adriano de las. 2001. *Le voyage en Chine d'Adriano de las Cortes S.J. (1625),* translated by Pascale Girard and Juliette Monbeig and with an introduction by Pascale Girard. Paris.

D'Elia, Pasquale. **[FR]**. 1942–49. *Fonti Ricciane. Documenti originali concernenti Matteo Ricci e la storia delle prime relazioni tra l'Europa e la Cina (1579–1615).* 3 vols., Rome.

Fatica, Michele, ed. 1996. *Matteo Ripa. Giornale (1711–1716) Volume 2.* Naples.

Golvers, Nöel ed. 2017. *Letters of a Peking Jesuit: The Correspondence of Ferdinand Verbiest, SJ (1623–1688). Revised and Expanded.* Leuven.

Kangxi Renhe xianzhi (康熙) 仁和縣志 (Renhe County local gazetteer). Kangxi edition, seventeenth century.

Kircher, Athanasius. 1987 [or. ed. 1667]. *China Illustrata. Translated by Charles D. Van Tuyl from the 1667 original Latin edition.* Muskogee OK.

Li, Zhizao 李之藻 ed., 1965 [or. ed. 1626]. *Tianxue chuhan* 天學初函 (First Collection of Celestial Studies), Taipei.

[Magalhães, Gabriel de SJ.]. 1649?. "Apontamentos do modo de viver e proceder do Padre João Adão nesta Corte...," Letter to visitor and vice-provincial of China, ARSI, *Japonica Sinica* 142, no. 32, ff. 1r-10v; published in Pih 1979: 319–48.

Margiotti, Fortunato, ed. 1975. *Sinica Franciscana. Relationes et epistolas Fratrum Minorum Hispanorum in Sinis, qui annis 1684–92 missionem ingressi sunt.* Vol. 8, in 2 tomes. Rome.

Martini, Martino. 1654. *De bello Tartarico.* Antwerp: Ex Officina Plantiniana Balthasaris Moreti.

Martini, Martino. 1998. *Opera omnia. Vol. 1. Lettere e documenti,* edited by Giuliano Bertuccioli. Trento.

Martini, Martino. 2013. *Opera Omnia. Vol. 5. De Bello Tartarico Historia e altri scritti,* edited by Federico Masini, Luisa M. Paternicò and Davor Antonucci, Trento.

Padberg, John. 1996. *The Constitutions of the Society of Jesus and Their Complementary Norms. A Complete English Translation of the Official Latin Text.* Saint Louis, MO.

Schall von Bell, Johann Adam. 1942. *Relation historique: lettres et mémoires d'Adam Schall S. J.,* edited and translated by Henri Bernard and Paul Bornet, Tientsin.

Semedo, Álvaro. 1653. *Historica relatione del Gran Regno della Cina.* Rome.

Spence, Jonathan, Janet Chen, Pei-kai Cheng, and Michael Lestz, eds. 2013. *The Search for Modern China. A Documentary Collection. Third Edition.* New York.

Standaert, Nicolas, Adrian Dudink and Nathalie Monnet eds. **[CCT BnF].** 2009. *Faguo guojia tushuguan Ming-Qing Tianzhujiao wenxian* 法國國家圖書館明清天主教文獻 – *Chinese Christian texts from the National Library of France – Textes chrétiens chinois de la Bibliothèque nationale de France.* 23 vols. Taipei.

Tacchi-Venturi, Pietro, ed. **[OS].** 1911. *Opere Storiche del P. Matteo Ricci, S.I. Edite a cura del Comitato per le Onoranze Nazionali, Vol. 2. Le Lettere della Cina (1580–1610) con appendice di documenti inediti.* Macerata.

Valignano, Alessandro. 2011 [or. ed. 1946]. *Il cerimoniale per i missionari del Giappone: Advertimentos e avisos acerca dos costumes e catangues de Jappão: importante documento circa i metodi di adattamento nella missione giapponese del secolo XVI: testo portoghese del manoscritto originale, versione letterale italiana. Nuova edizione anastatica con saggio introduttivo di Michela Catto,* Rome.

Verbiest, Ferdinand. 1938. *Correspondance de Ferdinand Verbiest de la Compagnie de Jésus (1623–1688) Directeur de l'observatoire de Pékin,* edited by Henri Josson and Léopold Willaert. Brussels.

Wyngaert, Anastasius van den and Georgius Mensaert, eds. 1954. *Sinica Franciscana. Relationes et epistolas Illmi. D. Fr. Bernardini Della Chiesa.* Vol. 5. Rome.

Secondary Sources

Alsteens, Stijn. 2014. "A Note on the Young Van Dyck." *Burlington Magazine* 156, no. 1331: 85–90.

Amsler, Nadine. 2018. *Jesuits and Matriarchs. Domestic Worship in Early Modern China.* Seattle.

Anonymous. 1924. "Une pratique liturgique propre à la Chine: Le Tsikin 祭巾 ou bonnet de messe," *Bulletin catholique de Pékin* 11:376–77, 404–6.

Astrain, Antonio. 1916. "Bonete de los Hermanos Coadiutores." In *Historia de la Compañía de Jesús en la asistencia de España. Tomo V. Vitelleschi, Carafa, Piccolomini*, 285–300. Madrid.

Bettray, Johannes. 1955. *Die Akkomodationsmethode des P. Matteo Ricci S.J. in China*. Rome.

Biermann, Benno. 1955. "War Martin Martini chinesischer Mandarin?" *Neue Zeitschrift für Missionswissenschaft* 11:221–25.

Bontinck, François. 1962. *La lutte autour de la liturgie chinoise aux XVII^ et XVIII^ siècles*. Louvain-Paris.

Borràs, Antonio. 1967. "En torno a la indumentaria de los Jesuitas españoles en los siglos XVI y XVII." *Archivum Historicum Societatis Iesu* 36:291–99.

Brockey, Liam Matthew. 2014. *The Visitor: André Palmeiro and the Jesuits in Asia*. Cambridge.

Brook, Timothy. 1998. *The Confusions of Pleasure. Commerce and Culture in Ming China*. Berkeley.

Cammann, Schuyler. 1944. "The Development of the Mandarin Square." *Harvard Journal of Asiatic Studies* 8 (2): 71–130.

Chang, Sheng-ching. 1998. "Das Porträt von Johann Adam Schall in Athanasius Kirchers *China Illustrata*." In *Western Learning and Christianity in China: The Contribution and Impact of Johann Adam Schall von Bell SJ*, vol. 2, edited by Roman Malek, Monumenta Serica Monograph Series XXXV-1/2, 1002–31. Sankt Augustin.

Dudink, Adrian. 2007. "The Holy Mass in Seventeenth- and Eighteenth-Century China: Introduction to and Annotated Translation of *Yu Misa Gongcheng* 與彌撒功程 (1721), Manual for Attending Mass." In *A Lifelong Dedication to the China Mission: Essays Presented in Honor of Father Jeroom Heyndrickx, CICM, on the Occasion of His 75th Birthday and the 25th Anniversary of the F. Verbiest Institute K.U. Leuven*, edited by Sara Lievens and Noël Golvers, 207–326. Leuven.

Ganss, George E. 1981. "Toward Understanding the Jesuit Brothers' Vocation, Especially as Described in the Papal and Jesuit Documents." *Studies in the Spirituality of Jesuits* 13 (3): 1–63.

Golvers, Noël. 2016. "Note on the Newly Discovered Portrait of Martini." In *Martino Martini: Man of Dialogue*, edited by Luisa M. Paternicò, Claudia von Collani, and Riccardo Scartezzini, 9–11. Trento.

Guillen-Nuñez, César. 2014. "The Portrait of Matteo Ricci: A Mirror of Western Religious and Chinese Literati Portrait Painting." *Journal of Jesuit Studies* 1 (3): 443–64.

Harris, George. 1966. "The Mission of Matteo Ricci S.J., a Case Study of an Effort at Guided Cultural Change in China in the Sixteenth Century." *Monumenta Serica* 25:1–168.

Hoey, Jack B. III. 2010. "Alessandro Valignano and the Restructuring of the Jesuit Mission in Japan, 1579–1582." *Eleutheria* 1 (1): 23–42.

Hsia, Ronnie Po-chia. 2002. "From Buddhist Garb to Literati Silk: Costume and Identity of the Jesuit Missionary." In *Religious Ceremonials and Images: Power and Social Meaning (1400–1750)*, edited by José Pedro Paiva, 143–54. Coimbra.

———. 2010. *A Jesuit in the Forbidden City. Matteo Ricci, 1552–1610*. Oxford.

Koch, Ludwig, ed. 1962 (photostatic reprint of Paderborn: Verlag Bonifacius-Druckerei, 1934). *Jesuiten-Lexikon: Die Gesellschaft Jesu einst und jetzt*. 3 vols. Leuven-Heverlee.

Levy, Evonne. 2011. "Jesuit Identity, Identifiable Jesuits? Jesuit Dress in Theory and in Image," in *Le Monde est une peinture: Jesuitische Identität und die Rolle der Bilder*, edited by Elisabeth Oy-Marra, Volker R. Remmert and Kristina Müller-Bongard, 127–52. Berlin.

Logan, Anne-Marie and Liam M. Brockey. 2003. "Nicolas Trigault, SJ: A Portrait by Peter Paul Rubens." *Metropolitan Museum Journal* 38:157–67.

Malatesta, Edward, and Francis Rouleau. 1994. "The 'Excommunication' of Ferdinand Verbiest." In *Ferdinand Verbiest (1623–1688): Jesuit Missionary, Scientist, Engineer and Diplomat*, edited by John Witek. Monumenta Serica Monograph Series XXX, 485–94. Nettetal.

Menegon, Eugenio. 1998. "I movimenti di Martino Martini nel Fujian (1646) in alcuni documenti inediti," *Studi Trentini di Scienze Storiche. Supplemento: Studi su Martino Martini*, LXXVII, Sezione Prima: 629–40.

———. 2006. "Deliver Us from Evil: Confession and Salvation in Seventeenth- and Eighteenth-Century Chinese Catholicism." In *Forgive Us Our Sins: Confession in Late Ming and Early Qing China*, edited by Nicolas Standaert and Ad Dudink, Monumenta Serica Monograph Series LV, 9–101. Sankt Augustin-Nettetal.

———. 2009. *Ancestors, Virgins, and Friars: Christianity as a Local Religion in Late Imperial China*. Harvard-Yenching Institute Monograph Series; 69. Cambridge, MA.

———. 2020. "'The Habit That Hides the Monk': Missionary Fashion Strategies in Late Imperial Chinese Society and Court Culture." In *Catholic Missionaries in Early Modern Asia: Patterns of Localization*, edited by Nadine Amsler, Andreea Badea, Bernard Heyberger, and Christian Windler, 30–49. London.

Muller, Jeffrey. 2016. "The Jesuit Strategy of Accommodation." In *Jesuit Image Theory*, edited by Wietse de Boer, Karl Enenkel, and Walter Melion, 461–92. Leiden.

Pavone, Sabina. 2013. "Spie, mandarini, bramini: i gesuiti e i loro travestimenti." *Il capitale culturale. Studies on the Value of Cultural Heritage*, no. 7: 227–47.

Peterson, Willard J. 1994. "What to Wear? Observation and Participation by Jesuit Missionaries in Late Ming Society." In *Implicit Understandings: Observing, Reporting, and Reflecting on the Encounters between Europeans and Other Peoples in the Early Modern Era*, edited by Stuart B. Schwartz, 403–21. Cambridge.

Philippi, Dieter. 2009. *Sammlung Philippi. Kopfbedeckungen in Glaube, Religion und Spiritualität*. Leipzig.

Pih, Irene. 1979. *Le P. Gabriel de Magalhães. Un jesuite portugais en Chine au XVIIe siècle*. Paris.

Rocca, Giancarlo ed. 2000. *La sostanza dell'effimero. Gli abiti degli ordini religiosi in Occidente*. Rome.

Romano, Antonella. 2016. *Impressions de Chine: l'Europe et l'englobement du monde (xvie-xviie siècle)*. Paris.

Sanfilippo, Matteo. 1996. "Travestimento o tradimento? I missionari cattolici in Cina nei secoli XVI e XVII." *Miscellanea di storia delle esplorazioni* 21:113–23.

Sanfilippo, Matteo. 1997. "L'abito fa il missionario? Scelte di abbigliamento, strategie di adattamento e interventi romani nelle missioni ad haereticos e ad gentes tra XVI e XX secolo." *Mélanges de l'Ecole française de Rome. Italie et Méditerranée* 109 (2): 601–20.

———. 2000. "Adattamento e travestimento: l'abito religioso nelle missioni." In *La sostanza dell'effimero. Gli abiti degli ordini religiosi in Occidente*, edited by Giancarlo Rocca, 113–18. Rome.

Schütte, Josef. 1980–85 [or. German ed. 1951]. *Valignano's Mission Principles for Japan*, 2 vols., St. Louis, MO.

Standaert, Nicolas. 1999. "Jesuit Corporate Culture as Shaped by the Chinese." In *The Jesuits: Cultures, Sciences, and the Arts, 1540–1773*, edited by John W. O'Malley and et al., 352–63. Toronto.

Vande Walle, Willy. 1994. "Ferdinand Verbiest and the Chinese Bureaucracy." In *Ferdinand Verbiest (1623–1688): Jesuit Missionary, Scientist, Engineer and Diplomat*, edited by John Witek, Monumenta Serica Monograph Series XXX, 495–515. Nettetal.

Väth, Alfons. 1991 [or. ed. 1933]. *Johann Adam Schall von Bell S.J., Missionar in China, kaiserlicher Astronom und Ratgeber am Hofe von Peking, 1592–1666*. Nettetal.

Wilkinson, Endymion. 2022. *Chinese History: A New Manual.* Fiftieth anniversary edition, revised and expanded in 2 volumes. Sixth edition. Cambridge, MA.

Zampol D'Ortia, Linda. 2016. "Purple Silk and Black Cotton: Francisco Cabral and the Negotiation of Jesuit Attire in Japan (1570–73)." In *Exploring Jesuit Distinctiveness. Interdisciplinary Perspectives on Ways of Proceeding within the Society of Jesus,* edited by Robert Aleksander Maryks, 137–55. Leiden.

Chapter 5

Masks in the Tropics: Performing Whiteness in Janet Schaw's *Journal of a Lady of Quality*

Manuela Coppola[1]

TRAVEL NARRATIVE HAS SHAPED THE REPRESENTATION of the West Indies, delivering to a western audience an image characterized, since the early accounts of the region, by lush and idyllic natural landscapes. In Aisha Khan's words, "the Caribbean has long been presented, and understood, as a literal and metaphoric arboretum, a crucible of the wildness and beauty of nature."[2] The focus on an Edenic yet perilous natural imagery represents for Khan a powerful epistemology that has informed the way the region has been known, a place "where nature becomes Nature – the region's *raison d'être* and common denominator."[3] By knowing the Caribbean through the lens of nature, European travelers have invariably depicted the natural and human landscape as irredeemably other, serving the metropolis's "obsessive need to present and re-present its peripheries and its others continually to itself."[4] Travel narratives then can also be seen as "portraits in the mirror," as Khan has suggested, "likenesses purportedly of the other yet reflecting multiple diffractions of the self."[5] While she argues that, in terms of the colonial gaze, the difference between portrait and self-portrait is debatable "since each is so profoundly implicated in the other,"[6] this is particularly true in the case of white metropolitan travelers depicting the white West Indian community in the eighteenth century. What happens when the object of the colonial white gaze is disturbingly similar to the self *but not quite?* When the tropical white "other" is neither black nor fully white?

This essay focuses on a context of creolization and material and cultural ex-

---

1. I wish to thank the editor of this volume, Elizabeth Goldsmith, for her thoughtful reading and helpful suggestions. I am also thankful to the Travel Literature Research Group at Boston University for the insightful conversations that have inspired this chapter.
2. Khan 2003, 93.
3. Khan 2003, 93.
4. Pratt 1992, 6.
5. Khan 2003, 95.
6. Khan 2003, 95.

change, wherein the instability and impermanence of whiteness was reflected in white metropolitan travelers' accounts of creole women's white masks. The travel narrative of Janet Schaw, a Scottish lady traveling to the West Indian islands of Antigua and St. Kitts and to North Carolina in the 1770s, provides an illuminating example of the ways in which the white creole community in the tropical colonies has been racialized and othered in the British imagination. The tropical weather, the proximity to the enslaved black population and the ensuing fears of miscegenation and cultural contamination, all contributed to a narrative that created the myth of the white creole as degenerate. As creolization – seen as a medical and cultural process – was being perceived as a threat to what Kathleen Wilson has termed the "nascent ethnicity"[7] of Englishness, by the eighteenth century "wealthy planters represented forms of vulgarity, backwardness and degeneracy that inverted the standards of English civility and culture."[8] A place of "ineffable otherness," the Caribbean became "the secret underground self"[9] of English society, while the white creoles were merely and unsuccessfully mimicking a white identity.

In her late eighteenth-century *Journal of a Lady of Quality*, Janet Schaw delivers a representation of white creole women that implicitly unmasks their otherness, like a distorted reflection in the mirror of metropolitan identities. As she repeatedly praises their qualities, depicting them as flawless models of domestic virtues, at the same time she reveals their obsession with material and discursive performances of whiteness, ultimately suggesting that their "white masks" expose, rather than conceal, their disturbing alterity. As Schaw's travel narrative addresses British anxieties over white "others" in the Atlantic colonies — white independentists in the North American colonies and white degeneracy in the West Indian colonies – this essay attempts to show how Schaw consolidates her own identity as white metropolitan woman while exposing the precarious identity of creole women as – unrefined, uneducated – white subjects.[10]

7. Wilson 2003, 13. In her words, "Englishness itself had emerged by the 1760s and 1770s as a nascent ethnicity that, although certainly defined through government, institutions and language, and sharing important features with European and Celtic cultures, still had within it what we would recognize as racialized assumptions, which ranged from the superior capacity of English people for rational thought to the greater aesthetic beauty of the 'pink and white complexion.'"

8. Hall 2018, 36. With the rise of the abolitionist movement in Britain in the 1780s, images of white creole inhumanity and cruelty proliferated.

9. Wilson 2003, 130. In Wilson's words, "Literally and figuratively, islands of slavery, exploitation and physical and social death, they seemed to promise obliteration for the enslaved, the penurious, and the prosperous alike."

10. Her travel narrative has attracted the attention of scholars for its relevance as a historical document of the early stages of the American revolution, as well as for her account of the white community of planters and slaveowners on St. Kitts and Antigua.

MATERIAL EXCHANGES, CREOLIZATION AND WHITE ANXIETY

During his voyage to the islands of Dominica and St. Vincent between 1765 and 1773–75, Italian painter Agostino Brunias was commissioned by his patrons to do a series of colonial scenes. One of these patrons was Sir William Young, Commissioner and receiver for sale of lands in Dominica. With his paintings, Brunias thus participated in the visual propaganda promoted in England to represent the newly acquired sugar colonies "as a place where raw materials and even people (...) could become cultivated and refined."[11] His delicate watercolors in fact portray finely dressed people of all shades engaged in buying groceries from a market or strolling in their parasols, offering to the European gaze an idyllic representation of a physically, socially, and culturally composite society, where slaves and free people of African, Carib, and European descent are depicted as living together in apparent harmony.

However, despite the efforts of colonial propagandists such as Brunias and many others, whether such endeavor was successful is a more debatable question. Although his paintings deliver a sanitized image of Caribbean life from whence any scene of slavery and its violence is carefully removed, his "ethnographic art" also mobilizes uneasy questions about whiteness and refinement.[12] In *Linen Market, Dominica* (ca. 1770), one of his many paintings depicting market life, a group of women are portrayed while shopping for linen at Roseau Sunday market. The sellers are mainly enslaved black women selling their provisions on their free day, while free and enslaved women of color as well as light-skinned women equally share this site of economic and social exchange. Although the social hierarchy of the plantation is by no means questioned by such exchanges, the scene would have nevertheless perplexed European observers. This, as well as many of Brunias's paintings, depicts women of different complexions and status sporting a range of fashion styles. European cuts and West African cloth, for example, are combined in different forms to shape a new creolized fashion. While African-Caribbean market women wear European full skirts and ruffs, Euro-creole women sport the light Indian muslin exchanged in West African markets and more appropriate for the tropical weather.[13]

The fact that colored and light-skinned women alike could have access to virtually the same textiles – both participating as buyers in the dynamic site of the market – may have appeared to many Europeans as evidence that the white settlers, and especially the women, had "gone native." Moreover, art historians Kay Dian Kriz and Mia Bagneris have both offered a more nuanced reading of the

11. Kriz 2008, 44. See also Tobin 2011, 15–21 for a discussion of how Brunias aestheticizes the labor of slaves.
12. See Kriz 2008; Tobin 2011; Bagneris 2018.
13. Skeehan 2015, 118.

Figure 1. *Linen Market, Dominica* by Agostino Brunias. Yale Center for British Art. Public domain.

light-skinned woman in the painting, implicating her ambiguous racial identity. In Bagneris' words, figures like hers who "look" white, are provocative precisely because of the gap between "looking" and "being": suspended "in a racial limbo dictated by the material limits of painting, 'looking white' is the most that they can ever do."[14] In a context where sumptuary laws were routinely disregarded, white women were virtually indistinguishable from mulatto women. As a consequence, the cultural and visual masquerade of identities performed by creole ladies further jeopardized the already unstable borders of whiteness.

Such material exchanges and racial distinction as the ones visualized in Brunias's paintings contribute to amplify British anxieties over white settlers in the West Indies. According to Bagneris, in fact,

> The expression of such anxieties regarding dress and personal adornment indicates the extent to which the consumer items that had played an integral role in constructing and performing elite white identity in Britain could not function in the same way in the empire's island colonies.[15]

14. Bagneris 2018, 193.
15. Bagneris 2018, 199.

The wealth produced in the West Indies through raw materials like sugar, had in fact financially supported cultural artifacts in England, creating and promoting the "culture of taste," the world of manners, politeness, and aesthetics that rapidly replaced social rank in determining "the character and quality of the self"[16] over the course of the eighteenth century. As birth and rank stopped being the markers of one's position in society, the cultivation of good taste through refinement (of manners, taste, and objects) became a crucial tool to refashion English subjectivities. In this new economy of taste, the raw materials exported from the Caribbean colonies and manufactured in the colonial center increasingly provided social value to the emerging classes. However, exotic raw materials could not be simply enjoyed for their aesthetic value; they had to be "tamed," refined and transformed into objects of taste in order to acquire symbolic value – their entanglement with slavery carefully removed.[17]

As Schaw noted in her *Journal*, documenting her trip to Antigua and St. Kitts in 1774–75, "their sugar is monstrously dear (...) [because] they use none but what returns from England double refined, and has gone thro' all the duties." (99–100) While the refining process is certainly the consequence of strict colonial tax policies, it is also a compelling example of the ways in which raw materials produced in the colonies were refined in the mother country only to be transported back to the colonies and used as "tools of refinement."[18] As Kriz has pointed out, "[t]he West Indies was configured as a place where raw materials were extracted by slave labor, and the metropole as the place where they were refined, consumed, and exchanged – transformed into goods (...) that confirmed the polish of their owners."[19] In the construction of this opposition between the "uncivilized" colonies and the "refined" mother country, however, the thick network of material and cultural exchanges could only produce fully white, refined subjectivities *unidirectionally*. While the exchange, possession, and consumption of refined colonial goods and luxury items became the marker of class status in the colonial metropole, such material and cultural exchanges in fact did not prove to be equally effective in refining colonial subjects on the other side of the Atlantic. As Brunias's paintings uncannily reveal, access to consumer items and

16. Gikandi 2011, 18.
17. Gikandi points out that this process "needed censoring mechanisms, schemes that would keep apart what was unpleasurable so that it would continue to satisfy instincts and desires that had become integral to modern culture." As he explores the conundrum at the heart of the culture of taste, he argues that the morally and aesthetically unpleasant connection between taste and its objects, and their material origin in the trivial world of commerce and of slavery, had to be carefully removed in order to fully participate in this economy of taste. In a similar vein, Tobin 2011 and Kriz 2008 also address such censoring mechanisms in visual and literary representations of the West Indian colonies as idyllic and refined landscapes.
18. Kriz 2008, 4.
19. Kriz 2008, 4.

commodities was often available to white colonizers as well as to slaves and free people of color, thus blurring the boundaries between white and non-white subjects and casting doubts about the possibility of effective refinement of white people in the tropical colonies. If these transatlantic exchanges testify to an increasing social mobility in England that enabled whoever owned wealth (wherever it came from) to claim (an unquestionably white) status, on the other hand, refined items consumed in the tropical colonies failed to provide any stable marker of identity. As the market becomes "the site [...] where Anglophone aesthetics are deconstructed and reconstituted as 'creole,'"[20] the possession and fashioning of material objects start to signal the emergence of new subjectivities that, to English eyes, could only problematically fall within the category of "white."

CREOLIZATION AND THE RACIALIZATION OF WHITENESS

Material objects such as textiles, skirts, and turbans all concurred to disguise, hide, or simply confound racial boundaries in the West Indies. Perceived as "one perpetual masquerade party"[21] in which distinctions of status were virtually impossible, the market testified to the emergence of a creole society that puzzled and perplexed European travelers. In the West Indian context, in fact, the racial indetermination of creole identity has always eluded straightforward categorization, complicating the frail relationship between whiteness and Britishness in the tropical colonies. The very use of the term "creole" in the British colonies describes a common, shared experience in the New World rather than a racial category.[22] As a destabilizing and complex figure, the creole thus cannot fit in the binary articulation of European identities, escaping the clear-cut logic of black and white.

As Roxanne Wheeler has brilliantly illuminated, however, until the end of the eighteenth century, whiteness in Europe was a contested category that did not rely solely on complexion but was instead a complex social construct encompassing notions of morality, rank, climate, religion.[23] Cecily Jones aptly points out the irony of David Hume's assertion of the superiority of whiteness in his infamous 1748 essay "Of National Characters," arguing that "in the eyes of the English not all whites were equally white, and Hume's fellow Scots, along with the Irish and the Welsh, embodied a quality of whiteness that was less certain than was English

20. Skeehan 2015, 119.
21. Bagneris 2018, 198.
22. The *Oxford English Dictionary* entry for "creole" in fact defines the early West Indian use of the word as: "a person born and naturalized in the country, but of European (usually Spanish or French) or of African race: the name having no connotation of colour."
23. "Throughout the eighteenth century, older conceptions of Christianity, civility, and rank were more explicitly important to Britons' assessment of themselves and other people than physical attributes such as skin color, shape of the nose, or texture of the hair." Wheeler 2000, 2.

whiteness."[24] Writing about Jamaica and Scotland, respectively, in the last quarter
of the eighteenth century, Edward Long and Samuel Johnson both reflect on the
"'savage' past in Africa and the Highlands" to ultimately justify English rule and
confirm its benefits for both the Africans and the Scots. As she states the contribution of the Scottish Enlightenment to racial classification, Wheeler contends
that both Scotland and Jamaica were "colonies [that] helped produce a racialized
interpretation of Englishness."[25]

In the early days of the British colonies, the category of whiteness appeared
to intersect with class and gender and not necessarily relying on race: by the second half of the seventeenth century, white indentured labor in the American colonies was in fact largely adopted as an instrument of social reform "[t]o cleanse
English society of disorderly members."[26] Indentured servants from Ireland and
Scotland, as well as convicted people and prostitutes transported to the colonies,
would have hardly fit in the category as they lived at the margins of colonial society. Strongly encouraged by the proponents of overseas expansion, transportation
of political dissidents, convicted, poor people, and "loose women" to Barbados
and Virginia, especially, served the double purpose of providing cheap labor in
the struggling colonies and solving the problem of overpopulation and poverty in
England. While political dissidents and criminals were shipped to Barbados and
Jamaica to be transformed into useful plantation laborers, "loose" women in the
colonies would provide the planters with domestic laborers, sexual companions,
and reproducers of free labor.[27]

With the rise of plantation society and the steady increase of black enslaved
people from Africa, however, the status quo came to depend primarily on the
preservation of racial purity.[28] While it became increasingly vital to categorize
and preserve it, whiteness remained a porous notion both in racial and cultural
terms, perceived as an unstable marker of identity in the promiscuous plantation
society, and thus particularly elusive and impermanent in relation to women.[29] As
whiteness intersected with race and class, the role of white creole women in the
reproduction of this unstable category became crucial. Cecily Jones has pointed

24. Jones 2007, 24.
25. Wheeler 2000, 192.
26. Walker 2020, 34.
27. Walker 2020, 35.
28. See Jones 2007. Whiteness as a cultural construction, however, was a particularly shifting
signifier in the colonies. Being white in the West Indies was different from being white in the rebellious American colonies, as Janet Schaw's *Journal* shows. See also Coleman 2003, 170.
29. Whiteness thus conveys "slippery shades of otherness," in Felicity Nussbaum's words. Nussbaum 2000, 69–88. See Coleman 2003, for a discussion of the racialization of whiteness in the
1760s and 1770s and its relation to gender. Burnard (2006, 44–45) and others agree that the Tacky
rebellion of 1760 was the watershed moment when the British hardened their racial classificatory
system, making it more difficult for mulattoes to pass for "white."

out the conundrum of white women regulating and reproducing whiteness while at the same time also potentially diluting it, encapsulating a set of anxieties over cultural and biological contamination.[30] As a contested site of identity, the white woman's body in the tropics became a shifting signifier whose representation was paramount to the construction and reproduction of whiteness within plantation society. English-born slaveholder, colonial administrator, and historian Edward Long explicitly and repeatedly addressed his concerns about the preservation of whiteness in his *History of Jamaica* (1774), lamenting the unsettling intimacy of white women with their black servants, thus blaming them for failing to reproduce whiteness (both symbolically and biologically). Eighteenth-century European travelers to the West Indies unanimously concurred in representing white creole women as brown-faced indolent, lustful, uneducated, and mischievous creatures, showing how complexion, social mores, sexuality and use of sorcery were areas of concern over white creole women.[31] It is not a coincidence that all these areas were traditionally associated with black women. By reproducing the trope of "blackening" and going native, European commentators deployed these "black masks" to voice their fears about the social and cultural implications of white women's proximity with black women, identifying such intimacy as one of the most important factors in white people's biological, medical, and cultural "contamination" in the tropics. Racial identity, in fact, did not rely solely on skin color, as the cultural anxiety surrounding creole identity testifies. As Deirdre Coleman has argued, "the challenge for white West Indians lay in maintaining their whiteness against the numerous assaults of creolization, such as physical adaptation to the tropical climate, interracial sex, or the misleading signifiers of dress or fortune.'"[32]

The perception of the tropics as a place that possessed an intrinsic corrupting power further reinforced the notion of the mother country as a refined space as opposed to the uncivilized and unrefined colonies. Fears of miscegenation, cultural contamination, together with the notion of tropical diseases, contributed to the persisting stereotype of the physical and moral degeneration of the white creole.[33] The physician Charles Leslie, for instance, comments on his arrival to Jamaica in 1740, remarking how the "gay bloom" of the Britons is replaced there by a sickly appearance: "their complexion is muddy, their colour wan, and their bodies meagre; they look like so many corpses."[34] Creolization, however, as med-

30. Jones 2007.

31. This is an image widely popularized by several travel narratives, novels, plays, caricatures, and vignettes in eighteenth-century Britain.

32. Coleman 2003, 173.

33. "The climatic model of disease emphasized the overwhelming impact of the environment and suggested a casual relationship between the tropical climate and the West Indian character." Senior 2018, 131.

34. Quoted in Senior 2018, 131.

ical treatises seem to suggest, was a reversible process that could be effectively manipulated. While it is true that the term "creole" does not have a connotation of color, within colonial medical discourse "creole" refers to "an individual who has become creolized through the medical process of 'seasoning' or acclimatization to the tropics."[35] A temporary medical process that relies on external factors, creolization is thus a gradual acclimatizing that brings with it certain visible and cultural characteristics. However, if the white subject can become creole through seasoning, it can also be assumed that this process can be controlled and manipulated in order to reverse it and restore the long-lost whiteness of the subject. Long stays in Britain to restore the ladies' health and rosy complexion, the use of parasols, bonnets and masks to protect the skin from the effects of the sun, skin bleaching through caustic oils to remove freckles and brown spots – these are all whitening practices well described in the literature of the time.[36] Possibly more disturbing than a white person turning "brown," it is the reversible nature of whiteness that generates anxiety, as it exposes it as an unstable signifier that can be lost and regained. If whiteness is not a fixed, permanent signifier, it can then be achieved or, rather, performed – by assuming it and taking it off – and ultimately worn as a mask.[37]

TROPICAL LADIES AND WHITE MASKS

The impermanence and instability of the category of whiteness have certainly contributed to the cultural anxiety of the British in the West Indian colonies, reinforcing the belief in the corrupting power of the tropics. However, they have also served to consolidate the idea of a national identity at home, projecting onto the white colonial woman images of otherness and artificial whiteness. The epistolary journal of Janet Schaw, written in 1774–75 and only published in 1923 as *Journal of a Lady of Quality; Being the Narrative of a Journey from Scotland to the West Indies, North Carolina, and Portugal, in the Years 1774 to 1776*, provides an

35. Senior 2018, 19.

36. The most invasive and painful practice is skin bleaching, reported in several botanical and medical treatises, travel and historical accounts, and poems, and often referred to as a "cosmetic" practice that white ladies perform in secrecy. In his popular poem *The Sugar Cane* (1764), Thomas Grainger for instance refers to the use of the cashew nut's highly caustic oil "as a cosmetic by the ladies, to remove freckles and sun-burning; but the pain they necessarily suffer makes its use not very frequent."

37. As Jones (2007, 26) argues, "whiteness was performed through expressions of piety, morality, modesty and sexual virtue, and the careful application of often dangerous cosmetics to produce the desired 'whiter than white' complexion." However, while Jones claims that "Poor white women had to some extent "prove" their claims to whiteness if they were to retain and enjoy the privileges of that racial identification" (5), my contention is that even planters' wives had to constantly negotiate and perform their whiteness.

illuminating example in this regard.[38] A lady belonging to an old Scottish family of some standing, in her trip across the Atlantic, Janet accompanied her brother Alexander (Sandie), who was due to take up a colonial appointment as customs officer on St. Kitts, and delivered two young relatives, who had completed their education in Scotland, to their father, a North Carolina planter. This part of her journey would also give her the opportunity to visit her brother Robert in Wilmington NC, where he owned a small plantation.[39] In the letters that comprise her narrative, Schaw shares her impressions of the places she visits following the conventions of the time of sentimental writing, while always taking her "cultural baggage" with her: "her Protestantism in Catholic Portugal, her virtue of hard work to the luxurious West Indies, deep loyalties to the Crown in North Carolina, and the genteel qualities of true ladies to all places and at all times."[40] The circumstances of her journey are firmly located in the colonial world, and her religion, her class, her ethics, her manners, all contribute to confirming her place at the heart of the colonial enterprise. Her status secures her a considerable degree of freedom from rigid social norms, and her education allows her to entertain polite conversation with her (male) hosts on literature, philosophy, and tropical agronomy. However, far from being critical of slavery or patriarchal norms, Schaw fully enjoys the privileges deriving from her position, such as free mobility and more fluid social norms, while she provides unsympathetic depictions of enslaved black people as well as of poor white immigrants.[41] Schaw's depictions of enslaved people are infamously disturbing. As she uses the "language of aesthet-

---

38. Schaw 1775/1921. The manuscript of this journal had been accidentally found at the British Museum in 1904 by the editors under the title "Travels in the West Indies and South Carolina, 1774–75." The quarto volume was in the form of an epistolary, likely intended for circulation among family and friends, with no mention of the name of the author. The investigative work of the editors filled out the blanks accompanying the author and the names of the people mentioned in the MS. After the Andrews stumbled across the British Museum MS, two private copies appeared, claiming the title for the original: as the editors wrote in their Preface, "almost comically, [they] have been *masquerading*, like three Dromios, somewhat to the confusion and dismay, but also to the amusement, of some of the discoverers of the prize" (emphasis added). In this play of double and hidden identities, one of the private copies (owned by an Antiguan historian) identified the author as a Janet Schaw, a lady belonging to an old Scottish family of some standing born near Edinburgh and a distant relative of Sir Walter Scott. Little is known about the life of Janet Schaw before or after this journey, and there are no images of her. It can be assumed that she was educated in English (as was the custom of upper-class Scottish families) and that she was familiar with the Scottish Enlightenment.

39. Her plans to remain in St. Kitts, however, were frustrated by the onset of the American revolution – her brother never took up his position in St. Kitts and she sailed back to London from Boston via Lisbon.

40. Arch 2005, viii.

41. Western women travel writers occupy a complex space, as they can be agents of subversion and counter-discourse while at the same time being complicit with that system.

ics to harmonize the violently disharmonic elements of colonial society,"[42] like Brunias in his paintings Schaw disturbingly removes and aestheticizes the horrors of slavery, in the attempt to depict a refined and agreeable West Indian society.

At the onset of her journey, when she realizes that her party are not the only passengers on the ship, Schaw describes the Scottish emigrant families as "a disgusting sight" (28) and compares them to Swift's Yahoos, while also emphasizing her distance from her fellow Scottish passengers in terms of class.[43] Despite her drastic change of attitude and her switch to a pietistic mode supported by the sentimental realization of belonging to the same affective community, Schaw still situates herself as the upper-class traveler, relegating her lower-class fellow white passengers to a dimension of subordination and alterity.

Class is not the only category that undercuts and problematizes whiteness in Schaw's account. During her stay on Antigua and St. Kitts, Schaw offers a glimpse of the extravagant habits of the white community in the tropical colonies. She enthusiastically describes the display of wealth and generosity of her West Indian guests and depicts them as "kind and beneficent masters" (104). While her contemporary (mainly male) fellow travelers to the West Indies contributed to the long-lasting stereotypical portrayal of the white creole woman as degenerate and uneducated, in her account of the islands Schaw devotes much attention to describing her interaction with the white creole ladies whose hospitality, modesty and exemplary maternal qualities she constantly praises:

> As to the women, they are in general the most amiable creatures in the world, and either I have been remarkably fortunate in my acquaintance, or they are more than commonly sensible, even those who have never been off the Island are amazingly intelligent and able to converse with you on any subject. They make excellent wives, fond attentive mothers and the best housewives ever met with. (113)

Such hyperbolic characterization of domestic and social skills seems to contradict the prejudice against the infamously unrefined white creole women. In stark contrast with the depictions of other travelers that have contributed to their reputation in the mother country, and in opposition to the "luxurious and amorous" (113) men in the colonies, the ladies Schaw meets with are exceedingly moderate and reserved:

> [T]he women are modest, genteel, reserved and temperate. This last virtue they have indeed in the *extreme*; they drink

42. Bohls 1994, 365.
43. Coltman 2018, 55.

nothing stronger in general than sherbet, and never eat above
one or two things at table, and these the lightest and plainest.
The truth is I can observe no indulgence they allow themselves In, not so much as in scandal, and if I stay long in this
country, I will lose the very idea of that innocent amusement;
for since I resided amongst them, I have never heard one
woman say a wrong thing of another. This is so *unnatural*,
that I suppose you will (good naturedly) call it cunning; but if
it is so, it is the most commendable cunning I ever met with,
as nothing can give them a better appearance in the eyes of a
stranger. (113, emphases added)

The extreme temperance described by Schaw, however, immediately raises some
doubts about its authenticity. The excessive praise the Scottish traveler reserves
for the white creole women seems to imply a none-so-subtle criticism, suggesting that these women are only performing their roles as perfect "tropical ladies"
for her benefit, as if they were wearing a "white mask." The image of the "white
mask" in relation to whitening practices is borrowed from the well-known practice of skin bleaching in the tropical colonies. In John Singleton's long poem, *A
General Description of the West-Indian Islands* (1767), the poet warns the "fair"
creole women indulging in this painful whitening practice against the risks of
losing their native beauty should "the foul infernal mask"[44] go wrong. Similarly,
in *The New Cosmetic, or the Triumph of Beauty, a Comedy* (1790), written by the
actor and playwright Samuel Jackson Pratt under the name Courtney Melmoth,
a young creole woman strives to regain her lover by using a "new cosmetic" that
promises that "the skin will come off in a mask".[45] Both Melmoth and Singleton
refer to this painful bleaching as a "white" mask revealing an even darker face,
insinuating the inherently unnatural and even devilish nature of such practice.[46]
As she points out their "unnatural" behavior, Schaw's descriptions similarly reveal
the artificial nature of white creole ladies' qualities.[47]

44. Singleton 1767/ 1999, 309.
45. Pratt 1790.
46. "Before the skin or mask of the face comes off, it turns black, and the person so suffering
becomes an horrid spectacle." Singleton 1767/1999, 309. See Coleman 2003, and Gwilliam 1994
for excellent discussions of the implications of these "white skin/white masks."
47. Schaw is not unaccustomed to sharp criticism towards other non-British white ladies. In
the following chapters, she has ... scathing words for her sister-in-law, a native of North Carolina,
whom she describes in these terms: "her person is agreeable, and if she would pay it a little more attention, it would be lovely" (161). Despite her praise as "most excellent wife and a very fond mother"
(161), Schaw implicitly blames her for not being a good housekeeper when she offers that her own
English maid could teach her sister-in-law's North Carolina maid "the British method of treating
linens."

In line with other travelers' accounts of women's excessive moderation in the tropical colonies, Schaw also notes how they abstain from drinking altogether. During her first dinner on Antigua, she notices that while her landlady — an older lady married to a Scotsman — toasts gracefully to and with her guests, the other young ladies present only drink lime and water.[48] In response to the landlady's remark that this is the reason they are so "indolent and spiritless," thus reproducing the well-known stereotype, the creole ladies reply that "it is not the custom" to do so. On the other hand, Schaw comments: "The poor women, whose spirits must be worn out by heat and constant perspiration, require no doubt some restorative, yet as it is not the custom, they will faint under it rather than transgress this ideal law" (80–81). While she blames the tyrannical custom that deprives the ladies of the restorative power of spirits, Schaw does not miss the opportunity to remark that they are afraid to transgress what she calls an "ideal law ... that did not appear founded on reason." On her part, however, she chooses to rebel against this unreasonable custom and asks for a glass of "the best Madeira she has ever tasted."

Drinking becomes a marker of identity and difference from the colonial ladies she has met on the journey. Wittily playing with her Scotch nostalgia during the journey back, Schaw will later write: "I long for a drink of Scotch two penny" (128). The editors point out that "her Journal (...) shows [Schaw] to be a well-born Scotswoman, loyal to her country and her king, in her tastes and preferences an aristocrat, and in religious, social, and political views a typical member of the educated class in Scotland in the latter half of the eighteenth century."[49] As such, they contend that she sometimes aristocratically claimed exemption for herself by drinking wine. However, her attitude would rather seem to suggest that, because of her positionality as a metropolitan white woman, she could easily afford this transgression. As an unmarried, childless, well-to-do middle-aged Scottish woman, Schaw enjoys the privileges of her status, which also include more fluid social norms in her interactions with the white community. Her identity as an outsider and traveler from the colonial center in fact gives Schaw the luxury of some cultural transgressions the creole ladies could not afford. As a traveler from Scotland, she can easily assert her whiteness in the colonies. By projecting her whiteness through her metropolitan Britishness, Schaw's white identity can be worn comfortably in the tropics: her mask fits. But while she observes the failure of others to make the mask fit, she is able to unquestionably claim her own white

48. This custom is reported by Bryan Edwards in his *History, Civil and Commercial*, with a similar condemning tone: "In their diet, the Creole women are, I think, abstemious, even to a fault. Simple water or lemonade, is the strongest beverage in which they indulge" (1793/1819 vol. 2, bk. 4, chap. 4, page 12).

49. Schaw 1775/1921, 11.

privilege and her cultural superiority over the native creole ladies she meets with, surreptitiously exposing them for not being "white" enough.

Rather than a stable mark of identity, whiteness in the West Indies was perceived as an *achievement* for white women, as it was imperative to preserve (material and symbolic) whiteness from the racial and cultural contamination ensuing from creolization. Schaw's depiction of white creole women's obsession with cultural and material performances of whiteness clearly exposes their vulnerable and precarious identity as West Indian creoles, implying that the "white masks" they constantly wear ultimately reveal – rather than conceal – their irreducible otherness. They all perform whiteness to some degree; but while Schaw convincingly performs her role, the ladies fail to reproduce a version of white British femininity in the tropics. Schaw's Scottishness brings a "lesser shade" of whiteness that, in the late eighteenth-century West Indian colonies, is overwritten by the white creole's inherent blackness. Cast against the grain of an even lesser shade of whiteness, Schaw's white identity can be unquestionably claimed against the backdrop of the white creole community.

The most explicit performance of whiteness, however, is displayed literally by the creole ladies in their scrupulous concern for preserving their complexion. Again, in Schaw's words such obsession with whiteness in all its forms is brought to the extreme:

> [T]hey want only colour to be termed beautiful, but the sun
> who bestows such rich taints on every other flower, gives none
> to his lovely daughters; the tincture of whose skin is as pure
> as the lily, and as pale. Yet this I am convinced is owing to the
> way in which they live, entirely excluded from proper air and
> exercise. From childhood they never suffer the sun to have
> a peep at them, and to prevent him are covered with masks
> and bonnets, that absolutely make them look as if they were
> stewed. (114)

Several travelers and commentators have observed this practice, and some have noted that these veils and masks were at times rudely used by the ladies to stare in the faces of all they meet. The main purpose of constantly wearing masks and bonnets, however, was to protect their skin from the consequences of solar exposure, in order to achieve and preserve the sought-after whiteness that would (at least visually) validate their position of power in the tropics and distinguish them from the mulatto women. While it is true that these were widespread practices in Europe throughout the Renaissance, in the eighteenth-century colonial context they assume a particularly significant value in relation to strategies of colonial power and identity construction. Calling attention to the visible sign (or, rather, "fetish") of racial difference, white women in the West Indies are conscious that skin color "functions to naturalize colonial domination in the register of the visible,"[50] and purposefully use it to consolidate their precarious and unstable identity. Therefore, not only does the fear of losing their visible mark of identity confirm the porous and shifting nature of eighteenth-century articulation of race and citizenship. It also addresses the white's anxieties over the preservation of power relations through the safeguarding of their most conspicuous sign of privilege.

Schaw, however, boasts of being immune from these anxieties: "As to your humble servant, I have always set my face to the weather, wherever I have been. I hope you have no quarrel with brown beauty" (115). This bold statement has been read "as a proud declaration of a healthy and rational adherence to the middle way of British beauty, as opposed to an extreme and overzealous aspiration toward pure whiteness."[51] As a Scottish lady in fact, Schaw's brown beauty/brown mask suggests her emancipation from the pressure of conforming to metropolitan, English models of white femininity without jeopardizing her status as white subject.[52] By contrast, the white mask worn by creole ladies – their artificial lily pallor lacking the color of the English rose – is further evidence of their otherness, marked by their cultural and physical proximity with enslaved black and mulatto people.[53] As Edward Long remarks, the white creoles' practice of protecting their complexion with bonnets, turbans, and masks was in fact borrowed from free mulatto women; in this way, although their purpose was to emphasize the difference between black and white, these whitening masks achieve the opposite effect of denaturalizing whiteness and obliterating difference.[54] This is further confirmed by the fact that, when her young niece Fanny "who just now is blooming as a new blown rose, was prevailed on to wear a mask, while [they] were on [their] Tour," her color changed within a week, making Schaw worry that "in a few months [it] would have made her as pale as any of them" (114–15). As Fanny risks becoming "as pale as any of them," Schaw exposes the volatility of difference; far from being an effective "mask," these and other whitening practices rather paradoxically *reveal* the porousness and instability of whiteness instead of concealing it.

50. Bohls 1994, 386.
51. Coleman 2003, 179.
52. See Bohls 1994, 388.
53. Innumerable accounts, treatises and poems have commented on the white creoles' complexion in terms of white lily/English rose, thus visually setting them aside from the English ladies and casting them as a separate group.
54. Coleman 2003, 178. Long remarks that neither white creole women nor free mulatto women venture out "without securing their complexions with a brace of handkerchiefs; one of which being tied over the forehead, the other under the nose, and covering the lower part of the face, formed a compleat helmet." Long 1774, 413.

Quite interestingly, even her Scottish friend Lady Isabella Hamilton seems to have embraced the customs of the place: "Tho' the lily has far got the better of the rose, she is as beautiful as ever" (122). Her lily complexion is further emphasized by the presence of a mulatto girl "dressed like a Sultana" (124) whom Lady Isabella keeps as a pet and whose skin, as Schaw remarks, "is a fine contrast to the delicate complexion of her Lady." (124) As a plantation owner, fellow Scot Lady Isabella cannot afford the luxury of Janet Schaw's metropolitan brown beauty; on the contrary, she uses other women's brownness and blackness to reinforce her white privilege.[55] Her whiter than white face in fact also serves the purpose of visual signifier of power over the enslaved black people on her plantation: as she visits the boiling house with her friend, she suddenly reveals her face to the people working there. As Schaw explains: "There were several of the boilers condemned to the lash, and seeing her face is pardon. Their gratitude on this occasion was the only instance of sensibility, that I have observed in them" (129). Her white face is deployed here as talisman, and as a crafty manipulation of the enslaved that helps maintaining social order on the plantation.[56]

In these descriptions, race, sex and culture are equally at work to deliver a reassuring, tropical version of the English lady identity. An (excessively) fair complexion, temperance, and politeness all concur to the construction of a white femininity rooted in domestic virtues transposed into a colonial space. However, these masks of identity delivering a homogeneous narrative of creole virtues implicitly reveal their author's skepticism about the creole's successful performance of white identity. The tropical ladies Schaw describes during her travels to the West Indies in fact seem to confirm the distance that, in Mackie's words, lies "between the words 'Jamaican' and 'lady.'" As they abstain from drinking, indulge in spiritless languor, lack conversational skills, and shun the English rose from their complexion, these creole women appear to be "making an oxymoron out of the term 'Jamaican lady.'"[57]

CONCLUSION

Schaw is so confident of her identity as a white woman – a "lady of quality" as the editors dub her in the published version of her manuscript – that she does not need to perform her whiteness like the white creole women she meets in the colonies. While the latter struggle to represent themselves as "hyper white"[58] through a variety of strategies, both social and material, Schaw's white subjectivity seems

55. As Bohls argues, "skin colour forms part of a pleasing chiaroscuro whose aesthetic value reinforces the rightness of enslaving and silencing racial others" (1994, 385).
56. See Coleman 2003, 179.
57. Mackie 2006, 192.
58. Coleman 2003.

to be confirmed and reinforced by the encounters with these "tropical ladies" who wear whiteness as a mask to validate their precarious position of power and privilege.

In his discussion of Horace's texts in this volume, James Uden contends that Horace enjoys the "privilege of living unmasked," borrowing this formulation from James Johnson. Because of his free status, the poet "can be consistent with himself," gaining even greater power over the people he owns by being free from the restraints of concealment and dissimulation. Unlike Horace, Janet Schaw does not enjoy such privilege. On the contrary, her status and her unfettered mobility allow her to play with multiple identities. As she confidently puts on different masks, from white lady to brown beauty, Schaw enjoys greater freedom than the white creole women imprisoned behind the mask of whiteness. A Scottish woman traveling across the Atlantic, Schaw can perform a more fluid version of whiteness as she describes colonial women's efforts to artificially and permanently pursue a white identity. By projecting otherness into these tropical ladies, Schaw can confidently shift between multiple shades of white, both culturally and visually, while still representing herself as unquestionably white, unquestionably British, and unquestionably lady. She also suggests that the creole ladies' white masks cannot wash away the moral taints associated with creole life – lack of refinement, cultural contamination, slavery. As they strive to perform an unconvincing tropical version of an English lady, creole ladies still appear to be morally and visually tainted, as their grotesque white masks ultimately reinforce their difference from metropolitan subjects, unmasking – rather than concealing – their otherness.

BIBLIOGRAPHY

Arch, Stephen Carl. 2005. "Introduction to the Bison Books Edition." In *Journal of a Lady of Quality; Being a Narrative of a Journey from Scotland to the West Indies, North Carolina, and Portugal, in the Years 1774 to 1776*, by J. Shaw. Edited by E. Walker Andrews and C. McLean Andrews (1934). Lincoln, NE.

Bagneris, Mia. 2018. *Colouring the Caribbean: Race and the Art of Agostino Brunias*. Manchester.

Bohls, Elizabeth. 1994. "The Aesthetics of Colonialism: Janet Schaw in the West Indies, 1774–1775." *Eighteenth-Century Studies* 27 (3): 363–90.

Burnard, Trevor. 2006. "'*Gay and Agreeable Ladies*': White Women in Mid-eighteenth-century Kingston, Jamaica". *Wadabagei* 9 (3): 27–49.

Coleman, Deirdre. 2003. "Janet Schaw and the Complexions of Empire." *Eighteenth-Century Studies*. 36 (2): 169–93.

Coltman, Viccy. 2018. "Paper Trails of Imperial Trav(a)ils: Janet Schaw's *Journal of a Journey from Scotland to the West Indies*." In *British Women and Cultural Practices of Empire, 1770–1940*, edited by R. Dias and K. Smith, 51–71. London.

Edwards, Bryan. 1793/1819. *History, Civil and Commercial, of the British Colonies in the West Indies*. 5 vols. London.

Gikandi, Simon. 2011. *Slavery and the Culture of Taste*. Princeton.

Gwilliam, Tassie. 1994. "Cosmetics Poetics: Coloring Faces in the Eighteenth Century." In *Body & Text in the Eighteenth Century*, edited by V. Kelly and D. Von Mücke, 144–59. Stanford.

Hall, Catherine. 2018. "What is a West Indian?" In *West Indian Intellectuals in Britain*, edited by B. Schwarz. Manchester.

Jones, Cecily. 2007. *Engendering Whiteness: White Women and Colonialism in Barbados and North Carolina*, 1627–1865. Manchester.

Khan, Aisha. 2003. "Portraits in the Mirror: Nature, Culture, and Women's Travel Writing in the Caribbean." *Women's Writing* 10 (1): 93–117.

Kriz, Kay Dian. 2008. *Slavery, Sugar, and the Art of Refinement: Picturing the West Indies, 1700–1800*. New Haven.

Long, Edward. 1774. *The History of Jamaica, or, General Survey of the Ancient and Modern State of that Island: with Reflections on Its Situations, Settlements, Inhabitants, Climate, Products, Commerce, Laws, and Government*. 3 vols. London.Mackie, Erin. 2006. "Jamaican Ladies and Tropical Charms." *Ariel: A Review of International English Literature*. 37 (2–3): 189–219.

Mills, Sarah. 1991. *Discourses of Difference: An Analysis of Women's Travel Writing and Colonialism*. London.

Nussbaum, Felicity. 2000. "Women and Race: 'A Difference of Complexion.'" In *Women and Literature in Britain*, 1700–1800, edited by V. Jones, 69–88. Cambridge, UK.

Pratt, Samuel J. 1790. *The New Cosmetic, or the Triumph of Beauty, a Comedy*. London.

Pratt, Mary Louise. 1992. *Imperial Eyes. Travel Writing and Transculturation*. New York.

Schaw, Janet. 1775/1921. *Journal of a Lady of Quality; Being a Narrative of a Journey from Scotland to the West Indies, North Carolina, and Portugal, in the Years 1774 to 1776*. Edited by E. Walker Andrews and C. McLean Andrews. New Haven.

Senior, Emily. 2018. *The Caribbean and the Medical Imagination, 1764–1834: Slavery, Disease and Colonial Modernity*. Cambridge.

Singleton, John. 1767/1999. "A General Description of the West-Indian Islands." In *Caribbeana. An Anthology of English Literature of the West Indies, 1657–1777*, edited by W. Krise, 314. Chicago.

Skeehan, Danielle. 2015. "Caribbean Women, Creole Fashioning, and the Fabric of Black Atlantic Writing." *The Eighteenth Century.* 56 (1): 105–23.

Tobin, Beth. 2011. *Colonizing Nature: The Tropics in British Arts and Letters, 1760–1820.* Philadelphia.

Walker, Christine. 2020. *Jamaica Ladies: Female Slaveholders and the Creation of Britain's Atlantic Empire.* Williamsburg.

Wheeler, Roxanne. 2000. *The Complexion of Race: Categories of Difference in Eighteenth-Century British Culture.* Philadelphia.

Wilson, Kathleen. 2003. *The Island Race: Englishness, Empire and Gender in the Eighteenth Century.* London.

Chapter 6

A Parisienne Discovers China and Japan: Laure Durand-Fardel's *From Marseille to Shanghai and Tokyo, Tales of a Parisienne* (1879)

Mary Beth Raycraft

LAURE DURAND-FARDEL (1817–87) WAS ONE OF FEW nineteenth-century French women to visit Asia and to publish impressions of her trip. Her 1879 book, *From Marseille to Shanghai and Tokyo, Tales of a Parisienne*, is comprised of twenty-five lengthy letters sent to family members during the seven months she spent traveling in Asia in 1875–76. When her husband, well-known physician Maxime Durand-Fardel (1815–1899), accepted a medical mission sponsored by the French government to study health conditions in Asian trading ports, she decided to accompany him. Laure Durand-Fardel looked forward to a family reunion in Shanghai where their daughter Régine (1849–n.d.) and her husband Louis-Auguste Pichon (1838–1924), a physician for the French navy, were stationed at the time. In addition, she was intrigued by the images of China and Japan that were circulating in late nineteenth-century Paris and eager to see first-hand these places where customs and traditions seemed so different from those of Europe.

In September 1875, the couple boarded a steamship in Marseille bound for Shanghai. During their two-month voyage, they stopped in port cities including Naples, Suez, Singapore, and Saigon. Upon arriving in China, the couple spent three months in Shanghai, where they resided with their daughter and her family. Toward the end of their stay, they made a month-long excursion to Japan to visit the principal cities and tourist attractions. Throughout the trip, her husband undertook research and collected information and specimens for his reports.[1] While he concentrated on his official duties, Laure Durand-Fardel took on a series of identities as she performed as a French tourist, earnest correspondent, fervent collector, and keen social observer.

In connection with our volume's theme of masking, this essay explores two aspects of her intriguing letters. Although Durand-Fardel does not engage direct-

---

1. Maxime Durand-Fardel 1876; 1877.

ly with disguise, she adopts a series of different personas as a traveler and letter writer as she journeys from Marseille to Shanghai and finally, to Tokyo. Moving through public and private spaces, she tries out different roles to better see and understand the cultures she observes. My analysis of Durand-Fardel's travel experiences is informed by both Mary Louise Pratt's work on contact zones and Marie Paule Ha's investigation of nineteenth-century French women's navigation of intercultural spaces in French Indochina.[2] The first section situates Durand-Fardel's letters in the context of late nineteenth-century French fascination with Asian culture and the popularity of travel accounts focused on China and Japan. In the second section, I discuss her self-presentation as a letter writer and a worldly Parisienne whose writing reveals both her preconceived ideas and candid reactions to the people and places she encountered. In the final section, I examine her shifting roles as an engaged traveler in Shanghai and Tokyo. Durand-Fardel's letters trace her movement from a wide-eyed French interloper to a more thoughtful cultural observer intent on taking readers beyond the superficial images of Asia circulating in nineteenth-century France and uncovering the spaces, cultural practices, and rituals of everyday life.

DISCOVERING CHINA AND JAPAN: FRENCH NINETEENTH-CENTURY TRAVELERS' ACCOUNTS

At the time of Durand-Fardel's trip, French curiosity about the east was particularly strong for several reasons. The establishment of the French Concession in Shanghai following the Treaty of Huangpu (1844), marked an important shift in diplomatic, trade, and cultural relationships between the two countries.[3] From a practical standpoint, the 1868 opening of the Suez Canal greatly facilitated travel from Europe to Asia. Ships regularly departed from Marseille on the Suez-Shanghai-Yokohama line and this steady circulation between Europe and Asia sparked increasing curiosity within France about the history, religions, art, and material cultures of Asian countries. In 1853, the forced opening of Japan to the West and the later display of Japanese art and material culture at the 1867 Paris Exposition universelle, helped to set in motion the Japonisme artistic movement. By the 1870s, French poets, novelists, artists, and composers, including Judith Gautier (1845–1917), Jules Verne (1828–1905), Camille Saint-Saëns (1835–1921), and Claude Monet (1840–1926), were incorporating colorful references to China

---

2. See Pratt 1992, 7 for a description of the highly charged space of intercultural contact zones, and Ha 2014, 242–44 for a discussion of French Imperial homes as hybrid cultural sites.

3. See Maybon and Fredet 1929, for an overview of the establishment and administration of the French Concession between 1847 and 1929.

and Japan in their work.[4] Around this time, Parisian collectors began acquiring Asian furniture, antiques, and trinkets, which were sold in specialty shops, displayed in private homes, and later organized as museum collections.[5]

The increasing number and popularity of late nineteenth-century French travelogues showcasing China and Japan paralleled the cultural fascination with Asia.[6] Male writers dominated this genre and several of them published popular travelogues around the time of Laure Durand-Fardel's trip, including the Comte de Beauvoir's *Voyage autour du monde* (1868), Théodore Duret's *Voyage en Asie* (1874), and Émile Guimet's *Promenades japonaises* (1878).[7] Prior to the publication of Durand-Fardel's book, only two other nineteenth-century French women had published travel accounts centered on Asia. Catherine de Bourboulon (1827–1865), a Scottish woman who was the wife of the French ambassador to China, penned several articles in the early 1860's for the journal *Le Tour du Monde* documenting her trip by horseback and caravan from Shanghai to Moscow.[8] An unusual account was written by little-known author Fanny Loviot (n.d.). In her 1860 book, *The Chinese Pirates: My Captivity in the China Seas* (*Les Pirates chinois, ma captivité dans les mers de Chine,*) Loviot recounted a melodramatic and most likely fictional adventure in which she claimed to have been kidnapped by Chinese pirates.[9]

In contrast to other travelers' depictions of life in China and Japan, Laure Durand-Fardel's letters introduced a different kind of traveler. She was an educated, middle-class Parisian woman whose letters highlight aspects of Chinese and Japanese cultures that were often excluded from other accounts, such as details about domestic life, gender roles, fashion, and food.

Moreover, Durand-Fardel's role as a travel writer came about in an unexpected way. She had not published any other writing before the trip and had not intended to share her letters with the public. It was only upon the urging of family and friends that she decided to pursue publication of the letters.[10] Her letters thus

---

4. See Butcher 2006, for an analysis of Verne's use of Hong Kong and Shanghai as settings in *Le tour du monde en quatre-vingts jours* (1872) and *Les tribulations d'un Chinois en Chine* (1879). See Emery 2020, 143–46 for a discussion of Judith Gautier's japoniste novel *L'usurpateur* (1875). See Reed 2017, 62–68 regarding Saint-Saëns's japoniste opera *La princesse jaune* (1872) and Monet's painting *La Japonaise* (1876).

5. See Chang 2002, on the collections of Henri Cernuschi (1821–96), Edmond de Goncourt (1822–96), and Émile Guimet (1836–1918). See Emery 2020,163–214, regarding the collection and museum founded by Clémence d'Ennery (1823–98).

6. Chang 2002, 17–19.

7. Reed 2017, 26–30.

8. Lapeyre 2008, 169–71.

9. Lapeyre 2008, 13–19; Monicat 1996, 26–27.

10. Durand-Fardel 1881, vi.

fall into the category of what Bassnett describes as "texts written for private pur-poses that were later made public."[11] The path to the publication of the private letters remains a bit mysterious. The Durand-Fardel couple was well-connected in Paris intellectual circles, and their contact with poet Prosper Blanchemain (1816–79) may have helped to attract the interest of Hachette, the leading pub-lisher of French travel accounts at the time. Two editions of Durand-Fardel's book appeared in 1879 and 1881. Each edition opens with a preface written by a French critic who confirms the authenticity of the letters.[12] A map depicting Du-rand-Fardel's itinerary is also included in each edition so that armchair travelers could easily follow her route.

The book received positive reviews and critics marveled at Durand-Fardel's ability to gain access to settings not typically frequented by tourists, including homes, theaters, hospitals, and opium houses.[13] In *Le Charivari*, critic Paul Gi-rard alluded to the French obsession with Chinese and Japanese cultures and admired Durand-Fardel's ability to lead readers into settings that "tantalize the European imagination."[14] Writing in *Le Livre*, another critic pointed out the ex-ceptional quality of her perspective: "I would call attention to the fact that, as a woman and the spouse of an eminent doctor, she was able to enter places that no other European traveler has experienced -- backstage at the theater, hospitals, intimate family settings – nowhere else do we find the same material."[15] In *La Liberté*, a male critic echoed this praise, describing her collection of letters as "a charming work, brimming with wit from start to finish and richer than many others in original ethnographic details that would have passed unnoticed by our sex…"[16] From these reviews, it is clear that Laure Durand-Fardel's letters offered new information about Asia from the perspective of a Parisienne.

LAURE DURAND-FARDEL'S EPISTOLARY SELF-FASHIONING

The epistolary format of Durand-Fardel's text recalls earlier French women's experimentation with real and imagined travel narratives including Madame d'Aulnoy's (1652–1705) *Relation du voyage d'Espagne* (1691) and Françoise de

---

11. Bassnett 2002, 232.
12. Poet Prosper Blanchemain (1816–79) wrote the preface to the 1879 edition and journalist Ferdinand Baudry (1816–81) contributed one for the 1881 edition.
13. See Coppola's discussion of Janet Schaw (ca. 1731-ca. 1801) in this volume. Schaw, like Du-rand-Fardel, was able to circulate more freely and enjoy more fluid social norms due to her privileged status as an upper-class traveler.
14. Girard 1879.
15. L. L. 1883.
16. Kuntz 1881, 3.

Graffigny's (1695–1758) *Lettres d'une Peruvienne* (1747).[17] In Madame d'Aulnoy's animated letters from Spain, she exploits the flexibility of the epistolary form to incorporate a variety of literary elements, including fairy tales, dialogues, and digressions.[18] Graffigny created a fictional epistolary travel narrative featuring a young Peruvian female narrator who comments on social customs in France.[19] In the mid nineteenth-century, two French women travelers, George Sand (1804–76) and Pauline de Noirfontaine (1799–1872), chose the epistolary form to recount their real-life travels. In Sand's letters to friends from Italy compiled in *Lettres d'un voyageur* (1837), she moves easily between the genres of travel narrative, autobiography, philosophical meditation, and aesthetic manifesto.[20] Noirfontaine published six letters penned during her two-year stay in Algeria in her book *Un regard écrit. Algérie* (1856). In letters to friends back in Paris, she shared candid descriptions of the Algerian landscape and people as well as outspoken criticism of the French colonial regime.[21] Reading Durand-Fardel's letters against those of earlier French women travelers reveals how she also works the epistolary mode to her advantage.[22] The letter format offers her the ability to interweave elements including descriptive tableaux, spontaneous digressions, and cultural observations.

Durand-Fardel's dated missives show that she participated in an ongoing exchange of information with family members throughout the trip. In his preface to the first edition, Blanchemain admired her spontaneous and natural style and compared her letters to a "causerie" or an ongoing conversation with family members back in France.[23] Durand-Fardel addresses her elderly mother and adult children in the first letter dated September 26, 1875. She explains that her letters are intended to be circulated among them: "By writing just one letter to all of you, I will be able to quickly share with you my detailed impressions"[24] To

17. Goldsmith 2021, 209–10.

18. Critics continue to debate whether D'Aulnoy actually sent her letters or if she used the epistolary form as a conceit. See Hester 2007, for a thoughtful analysis of how D'Aulnoy interweaves stylistic and structural elements from different genres into her letters.

19. See Goldsmith 2021, 209 regarding Graffigny's use of a fictional narrator and outsider to French culture as a device to critique cultural practices.

20. See Thompson 2012, 272–83 for a discussion of the original structure and themes of Sand's *Lettres d'un voyageur* (1837).

21. See Yourcef 2020, 4–5, for an overview of Noirfontaine's letters and a summary of her criticism of the French colonial regime.

22. British traveler Isabella Bird (1831–1904) also published an epistolary account of her trip to Japan in 1880, *Unbeaten Tracks in Japan*. Although the book takes the form of a compilation of letters to her sister, Bird never actually sent the letters.

23. Laure Durand-Fardel 1881, vi.

24. Laure Durand-Fardel 1881, 1. All quotations are taken from the 1881 edition. The translations are my own.

keep her family informed of the different stages of her journey, Durand-Fardel adopted a disciplined practice in which she wrote letters in the evening to capture the most striking events of the day. Her letters can be divided into three groups. In the first ten letters, she described life onboard the ship including daily routines, interactions with other passengers, and short stays in port cities. The second group is composed of ten letters written during her three-month stay in Shanghai. The third group includes four letters written during her brief sojourn in Japan. In a final letter, penned just prior to her departure from Shanghai for the return trip to Marseille, she offered some final reflections on the trip.

In keeping with the subtitle of the book, *Tales of a Parisienne*, Durand-Fardel's early letters expose her self-fashioning as a patriotic Frenchwoman and a sophisticated Parisienne.[25] During stops in port cities, she relied heavily on her French network to help her both navigate and interpret what she was seeing. French diplomatic representatives welcomed the couple upon their arrival in each port and served as tour guides. When depicting the places she visited on route to Shanghai, Durand-Fardel leans into her Parisian identity and helps readers imagine the scene by evoking Paris streets and landmarks. She compares a bustling café in Port Saïd to the famous Parisian café "Tortoni" (33), a racetrack in Hong Kong to those of Auteuil and Longchamp (150), and the busy port of Canton to the late-afternoon traffic on the "rue de Richelieu" (220). Durand-Fardel's enthusiasm for shopping and collecting also helped to reinforce her image as a fashionable late nineteenth-century Parisienne.[26] Throughout the trip, she visited markets and shops and was thrilled to curate her own collection of authentic items that were not available in France at the time. In her letters, she provides family members with regular updates on her acquisitions: "we are buying continuously; our excuse is that we are surrounded by temptations and mindful of the value that these objects will acquire in France" (388). Unlike French antique and art dealers who were reselling items purchased in Asia for a profit, Durand-Fardel purchased souvenirs for family members and acquired items that she would later display in her Paris apartment as both vestiges of the travel adventure and evidence of her own sophisticated taste.[27]

As a Parisienne, Durand-Fardel generally keeps to a cultural script and evaluates other communities from a subjective position of polite Parisian culture. Her

25. Two other nineteenth-century travel accounts also include "Parisienne" in their titles: Adèle Toussaint-Samson, *Une Parisienne au Brésil* (1883) and Marie de Ujfalvy-Bourdon, *De Paris à Samarkand, Le Ferghanah, le Kouldja et la Sibérie orientale. Impressions d'une Parisienne* (1880).

26. See Emery 2020, 24–38 on the growing popularity of collecting for women in late nineteenth-century Paris, and 50–51 regarding the availability of Asian-inspired furniture and decorative arts in Parisian department stores.

27. The inventory of her Paris apartment at the time of her death includes descriptions of furniture, fabric, and jewelry purchased during the trip. See Durand-Fardel 1887, *Inventaire après décès.*

initial reactions to the local people she encounters are rooted in nineteenth-century French racial and ethnic stereotypes. Although she accepted prevailing colonial attitudes of the time and exhibited a Parisian sense of superiority in terms of manners, dress, and food, Durand-Fardel also viewed herself as the open-minded heroine of an adventure story. Equipped with limited prior knowledge of China or Japan, Durand-Fardel looked forward to learning on site and boldly summarized her goals as a traveler: "I came here to see, to experience, and to learn" (250). She recalled her childhood fondness for the tales of Robinson Crusoe and Captain Cook, calling them "the most colorful stories of my childhood" (56–57). When exploring port cities, she performed as an adventurer and displayed a lively sense of curiosity. Durand-Fardel was frequently struck by the hybrid, intercultural nature of places that had been colonized by the French, British, or Dutch. When not being chaperoned by a French official, she sought out authentic experiences and explored neighborhoods off the beaten track, sampled local food without hesitation, and fearlessly climbed into sedan chairs, wheelbarrows, and rickshaws (249). Instead of simply curating examples that confirmed European stereotypes, Durand-Fardel gathered first-hand evidence and shared vivid images of the people and places she encountered. Alternating between the perspective of a sophisticated Parisienne and that of an open-minded traveler, she attempted to understand and explain the values underlying the customs and behaviors she observed.

While confident in her perspective as a Parisienne, she repeatedly apologizes for her inexperience as both a traveler and a writer. Upon arriving in Hong Kong, she regrets that her limited travel experience influences her perspective: "You will perhaps find me too enthusiastic, but I have seen so little prior to today. Everything surprises me, everything is new, at each site, at each view of the horizon, I find myself repeating: 'I have never seen anything so beautiful!'" (137). When she tries to evoke landscapes, settings, and interactions, she often expresses frustration at her inability to accurately convey what she sees. For example, when Saigon comes into view from the ship, the idyllic scene surpasses her descriptive abilities: "I will never be able to give you an idea of the deliciously picturesque scene" (123). After circulating in the streets of Canton, she similarly finds herself at a loss for words: "How can I make you understand what my first hour in the streets of Canton was like? Where to begin and which expressions to use? Nothing seems to me to be sufficient" (155). In these comments, she takes on the role of a critic, finding her own writing insufficient to the task of describing remarkably different places and customs. To compensate for the limits of her traveler's gaze and writing ability, she promises to supply more details upon her return (233, 395). In this way, her letters function as a prelude to the more extensive conversations that she planned to have with family members upon her return.

Shifting Roles: From Tourist to Engaged Cultural Observer

In her letters from Shanghai, Durand-Fardel displays an increasing cultural awareness and a willingness to go beyond French attitudes to make sense of what she
observes. Although her letters still include spontaneous, unfiltered reactions, she
also begins to incorporate lengthy digressions that provide historical and cultural
context for her readers. During her stay in Shanghai, Durand-Fardel gained a
French insider's view of domestic and social life in the multicultural city and used
her letters as a forum for working out her ideas about a range of topics, including
funeral traditions, the custom of foot binding, and the complex relationships
between the Chinese and the Europeans living in Shanghai, Her interactions
both inside and outside of her daughter's house demonstrate her determination
to investigate settings rarely visited by tourists and to better understand Chinese
customs and traditions. Shifting from grandmother to tourist to shopper, she
embraces different roles as she moves between private and public spaces.

Durand-Fardel and her husband stayed with her daughter's family at their
home on Peking Road, which she described as "one of the most beautiful streets
in Shanghai" (246). Inside the house, Durand-Fardel found a hybrid setting
with French and Chinese influences. She was dismayed to hear her two-year old
granddaughter babbling in a mix of several languages (231) but pleasantly surprised to learn that the Chinese cook had been trained in French techniques and
prepared meals combining local products such as shark fin and Ningpo oysters
with delicate French sauces (309). Durand-Fardel's interactions with servants in
the house provide insight into the complex household relationships between the
French inhabitants and Chinese servants in late nineteenth-century Shanghai.[28]
As a devoted French mother and grandmother, she made it a priority to help her
daughter with childcare, food preparation, and management of household help.
She appreciated some members of the staff, particularly the wet nurse hired for
the infant grandchild: "a very kind young Chinese woman who always supplies
plenty of milk" (231). What she found most challenging was the powerful status
of the multilingual "boy" who served as translator, overseer, and purchaser of
goods:

> Now we have a boy, a kind of manager and supervisor of the
> servants who would not work otherwise. He oversees work-
> ers in the stable and the gardens, as well as the cooks and
> the coolies who work inside the house. He also does all the
> purchasing and is the *great thief* of the house; but the entire
> city is organized this way and it would be impossible to do it

---

28. See Ha 2014, 227–29, for a thoughtful analysis of the uneasy rapport and mutual distrust
between French women and servants in the French colonies.

> differently mainly because of the language. The head boy is
> the one employee who understands and speaks both English
> and French while the other servants only understand Chinese
> (246–47).

Durand-Fardel comments show that she quickly grasped the critical importance of language skills in the multi-cultural environment of Shanghai. While she judged it best to respect the servant hierarchy within the household, her comments suggest the ongoing mistrust between the French family and the Chinese servants.

Outside of the house, Durand-Fardel felt very much at home in Shanghai's French concession, where Paris-style society life was in full swing.[29] She settled into a social routine that included carriage rides on fashionable Bubbling Well Road and participated in visits, dinners, and balls organized by French, British, and American acquaintances living in the foreign concessions. In contrast to other European visitors who confined their movement and activities to the foreign concessions, Durand-Fardel's natural curiosity led her to explore other areas of Shanghai. Eager to learn more about the history and culture of the city, she went on guided excursions with local French experts. Her visits to numerous Buddhist temples led her to incorporate digressions on Chinese religions into her letters (293–95). During a walk on the outskirts of Shanghai, her discovery of a field filled with coffins prompts her to engage in a discussion of funeral traditions (261–62). During these touristic visits, Durand-Fardel became increasingly aware of spatial and cultural tensions between the Chinese and the inhabitants of the foreign concessions. For example, after providing an overview of funeral practices, she points out that the local Shanghai population had protested the proposed construction of a road by the European authorities as it would have disturbed an area where coffins were located (263). In a similar example, she describes tensions surrounding the installation of a railroad line by a British company and the anger of the local Chinese authorities (311).[30]

As she became more comfortable circulating in Shanghai, Durand-Fardel sought to distinguish herself from other Europeans living in the city. Curious about the old walled city that shared a border with the French Concession, she and her husband cautiously ventured there: "We set out, a bit hesitant as we were slightly troubled by the tales we had heard and not certain that we would return home safely. But this impression disappeared as soon as we entered through the

---

29. See Kang 2018, 53–54, for a discussion of how the French Concession was organized and administered to promote a French way of life in this sector of Shanghai.

30. Interestingly, in the 1881 edition of her book, she added a footnote indicating that the British railroad project in Shanghai had been abandoned in the face of the Chinese authorities' opposition (411).

door: people gathered around us out of curiosity but gave no indication of bad feelings and I noticed the kindness in their facial expressions" (277). Inside the walls of the old city, Durand-Fardel and her husband were surprised to encounter a very different Shanghai with a mix of languages, outgoing merchants, and shops piled high with trinkets. They began frequenting the shops and engaged multi-lingual Chinese boys to help them bargain with merchants for lower prices (279). Eventually the couple developed such a friendly rapport with the merchants that they no longer felt like outsiders (313). Although these relationships were clearly anchored in transactional exchanges, Durand-Fardel's ongoing contact with local merchants was unusual and distinguished her from other French tourists and acquaintances in the Concession.

The couple's successful forays into the old city emboldened Durand-Fardel and her husband to visit other settings outside of the French Concession including tea shops, theaters, and opium houses. In her letters, she adopts an increasingly self-assured tone as she offers animated descriptions of the layout, décor, and people she encounters in these spaces. Taking on the role of a cultural insider, Durand-Fardel introduces other Europeans to the shops and teahouses of the old city (296). Unlike their European friends in Shanghai, Durand-Fardel and her husband attended the theater and visited an opium house. At the theater, Durand-Fardel was surprised to learn that women's roles were always played by men and admired the costumes, creative staging, and dramatic plots. (303–04). In a description of a visit to an opium house, she provides an overview of the layout, personnel, and clients:

> They are similar in layout to a shop but are divided into
> smaller rooms where square beds line the walls. At the
> entrance, there is a counter where the master of the place dis-
> tributes small balls of opium that he takes from small jars, like
> those used by our pharmacists for hair pomade. Stretched out
> on the beds are individuals who are either sleeping or maneu-
> vering their pipe… (289).

Through these excursions into settings rarely frequented by other Europeans, Durand-Fardel provides first-hand descriptions in which she demystifies these places and practices.

Throughout her letters, Durand-Fardel was very attentive to Chinese women's appearance and beauty practices.[31] Admiring their carefully groomed hair, dramatic makeup, and the richly embroidered fabrics of their robes and slippers, she was thrilled to encounter Chinese women in person. Durand-Fardel

---

31. See Goldsmith's discussion in this volume regarding travelers' long-standing interest in observing and commenting on women's beauty.

was especially intrigued by the custom of foot-binding. Like other Europeans, Durand-Fardel was puzzled by this tradition, which was painful and disfiguring yet in Chinese culture so charged with both erotic and socio-economic connotations.[32] While attending a lunch at a home in Canton, she observed with great interest an elegantly dressed Chinese woman who awkwardly made her way across the room: "We saw an attractive young woman tottering on her tiny feet, as if trying to cross a stream without falling into the water" (199). This unusual spectacle leads Durand-Fardel to seek out an opportunity to view a naked foot, unbound from its layers of fabric. After numerous obstacles, Durand-Fardel leveraged her French network to negotiate a viewing of the unwrapping of a young Chinese woman's bound foot at a French Catholic hospital in Shanghai. In this unsettling scene, a group of Chinese and French women watch as the young woman reluctantly removes the many layers of fabric covering the foot. Durand-Fardel's theatrical description, filled with uncomfortable suspense, signals her determination to cross boundaries to witness what others had never seen. At the sight of the naked foot, Durand-Fardel expressed both horror and sympathy: "an awful deformity that inspires great compassion for the unfortunate women who are destined to undergo this type of treatment" (405). This gesture of unmasking the foot veiled in layers of delicate silk, allows her to expose the gruesome reality of this practice. By reporting on the appearance of the deformed foot, she hoped that this direct evidence might help mobilize more support in the movement to ban this practice.

After spending three months in Shanghai, Durand looked forward to a month-long tour of Japan. Durand-Fardel's excursion to Japan allowed her to once again embrace her identity as a well-connected French tourist and enthusiastic shopper. Along with her husband and daughter, she took a ferry from Shanghai to Nagasaki. The group then toured Osaka, Tokyo, and Yokohama with French dignitaries. In her letters, she sets up a series of comparisons between Japan and China and emphasizes the differences between these two cultures. Her impressions of Tokyo are especially telling in terms of late nineteenth-century connections between Japan and Europe. Arriving in the center of the city, she was surprised to see European-style architecture and wide, freshly paved streets that reminded her of Paris (358). The juxtaposition of traditional local architecture and newer European-style buildings leads her to digress on the strong collaboration between Japan and France following the Meiji Restoration in 1868. She learns from her French guide that Japan's leaders relied on French models and

32. See Meng 2021, 21 for an overview of the history and practice of foot binding. At the time of Durand-Fardel's visit, the practice had been condemned by Chinese and European critics but would not be outlawed until 1912. It is possible that Laure Durand-Fardel's interest in foot binding was inspired by her husband's ongoing research on Chinese courtesans and his observation that those with bound feet were in great demand. See Maxime Durand-Fardel 1876, 12.

support when modernizing political institutions, urban design, architecture, and technology during this period (352–53). Interestingly, as the tour group headed toward the Summer Palace, they encountered a man dressed in traditional samurai clothing, bearing two swords. Their French guide took advantage of this unexpected meeting to give an overview of the momentous changes in Japan's political and social structure with the overthrow of the military government of the Tokugawa Shogunate (1603–1868) and the Meiji Restoration (1868) (354).[33] At the Summer Palace, Durand-Fardel and the other French visitors were welcomed into the lavish interior and served tea by a roaring fire (356). Within the refined atmosphere of the palace, furnished with French furniture and decorative objects, Durand-Fardel experienced a hybrid space that communicated the strength of the diplomatic relationship between France and Japan.

Durand-Fardel also saw evidence of French influence when she boarded a train bound for Osaka at the modern station in Nagasaki. In contrast to the ongoing disputes in Shanghai regarding the installation of a Western-style railroad line, the Japanese seemed more open to modern technology. The appearance and the efficiency of the station reminded her of those in France: "It is so surprising to find myself here, as if in the middle of France, with waiting rooms, employees and guards wearing French uniforms, but it is even more elegant and everything seems very European except for the Japanese characters and the language (329).

Given her limited personal contact with Japanese men and women, Durand-Fardel drew conclusions about the culture based mainly on what she observed in public settings. In descriptions of Japanese women, she focuses primarily on their movement and ability to circulate in the city. Despite the narrow cut of their restrictive robes, she notices that Japanese women circulate in public more freely than Chinese women (319–20). She also points out that the most distinctive and unsettling feature of Japanese women is their blackened teeth (392–93). Durand-Fardel declares that she is confident, however, that women will abandon this repulsive practice with increasing contact with Europeans (393).

After visiting both the men's and the women's theaters in Yokohama, Durand-Fardel offered a comparison of Japanese and Chinese theater architecture and practices. She preferred the Japanese theater layout, costumes, and set design and was better able to grasp the plot in contrast to the more complex plays that she had attended in Shanghai. As their trip to Asia was nearing a close, the Durand-Fardel couple indulged in last-minute shopping in Yokohama: "Whenever we are not doing a cultural visit or attending a social event, we spend our time picking up souvenirs. But there are so many beautiful items that we regret that we cannot buy them all. Nevertheless, our collection is becoming very respect-

33. See Sims 2001, for a comprehensive overview of this transitional period.

able" (382). In fact, their acquisitions were so numerous that when it came time to pack for the return trip to Shanghai, they devised a strategy to avoid customs duties by packing their purchases in their luggage and filling the many cartons with clothing and fruit (382–83).

In her last letter from Japan, she presents one final comparison between the two countries. Weighing the similarities and differences between the two cultures, she accentuates their distinct attitudes toward Europeans. From her perspective, the Japanese appeared to embrace European influence on many levels while the Chinese showed outright contempt:

> The enchanting appearance of tourist sites, the splendor of the vegetation, the good humor of the population, their apparent wealth, and finally the warmth with which they accept our customs, contrasts vividly with the severity of the Celestial Empire and the disdain that the Chinese have for contact with our civilization (379).

At the end of her trip, Japan's openness to European ideas of modernization clearly appealed to and reinforced her Eurocentric view of the world.

In conclusion, Laure Durand-Fardel's travel experience and letters offered her an opportunity to reinvent herself as she gradually became at ease navigating new settings and communicating her impressions and opinions. Assuming the identities of an inquisitive traveler, a faithful correspondent, an enthusiastic shopper, and cultural observer, she skillfully circulated in the culturally complex urban spaces of Shanghai and Tokyo. In her final letter, written as she prepared to head back to Marseille, Durand-Fardel admitted that her Asian sojourn had left her with mostly superficial impressions (401). In the end, however, what she viewed as naive observations result in a vivid documentary of travel and intercultural connections in late nineteenth-century China and Japan from a first-time travel writer. Her letters add to the story of nineteenth-century French fascination with China and Japan and reveal a traveler who boldly crossed cultural and spatial boundaries to demystify for French readers some of the mystery surrounding late nineteenth-century Chinese and Japanese cultures.

Bibliography

Aulnoy, Marie-Catherine Le Jumel de Barneville, comtesse d'. 2022. *Travels into Spain*. Edited and translated by Gabrielle M. Verdier. New York.

Bassnett, Susan. 2002. "Travel Writing and Gender," in *The Cambridge Companion to Travel Writing*. Edited by Peter Hulme and Tim Youngs, 225–41. Cambridge.

Beauvoir, Ludovic de. 1872. *Voyage autour du monde*. Paris.

Bird, Isabella. 1880. *Unbeaten Tracks in Japan*. London.

Bourbelon, Catherine de. 1991. *L'Asie cavalière: de Shanghai à Moscou 1860–62*. Edited by Chantal Edel and Robert Sctrick. Paris.

Butcher, William. 2006. "The Tribulations of a Chinese in China: Verne and the Celestial Empire." *Journal of Foreign Languages* 5:63–78.

Chang, Ting. 2002. "Collecting Asia: Théodore Duret's *Voyage en Asie* and Henri Cernuschi's Museum." *Oxford Art Journal* 25 (1): 17–34.

Durand-Fardel, Laure. 1881. *De Marseille à Shanghai et Yedo, récits d'une Parisienne*. Paris.

———. *Inventaire après décès*, 1887. 3 octobre 1887, Archives nationales, Paris, Cote MC/ET/LXVIII/1493.

Durand-Fardel, Maxime. 1876. *La vie irrégulière et la condition des femmes en Chine*. Paris.

———. *La lèpre en Chine*. 1877. Paris.

———. *Une mission médicale en Chine*. 1877. Paris.

Emery, Elizabeth. 2020. *Reframing Japonisme: Women and the Asian Art Market in Nineteenth-Century France, 1853–1914*. London.

Girard, Paul. 1879. "Une Parisienne en voyage." *Le Charivari*, 15 mars 1879.

Goldsmith, Elizabeth C. 2021. "Epistolary Fiction: The Novel in the Postal Age." In *The Cambridge History of the Novel in French*, edited by Adam Watt. Cambridge.

Graffigny, Françoise de. 2009. *Letters of a Peruvian Woman*. Translated by Jonathan Mallinson. New York.

Guimet, Émile. 1878. *Promenades japonaises*. Paris.

Ha, Marie-Paule. 2014. *French Women and the Empire: The Case of Indochina*. Oxford.

Hester, Nathalie. 2007. "Travel and the Art of Telling the Truth: Marie-Catherine d'Aulnoy's Travels to Spain." *Huntington Library Quarterly* 70 (1): 87–102.

Kang, Mathilde. 2018. *Francophonie and the Orient: French-Asian Transcultural Crossings (1840–1940)*. Amsterdam.

Kuntz, P. 1881. "Le pied des Chinoises." *La Liberté*, 26 juillet 1881, 3.

L. L., Ch. 1883. "De Marseille à Shanghai et Yedo." *Le Livre*, 10 février : 111.

Lapeyre, Françoise. 2008. *Le roman des voyageuses françaises (1800–1900)*. Paris.

Loviot, Fanny. 1860. *Les pirates chinois: ma captivité dans les mers de Chine*. Paris.

Maybon, Charles, and Jean Fredet. 1929. *Histoire de la Concession française de Shanghai*. Paris.

Meng, Qingya. 2021. "Le confinement des femmes chinoises à travers les récits de voyageurs français au dix-neuvième siècle." *TraHs* 9:9–26.

Monicat, Bénédicte. 1996. *Itinéraires de l'écriture au féminin: voyageuses du dix-neuvième siècle*. Amsterdam.

Noirfontaine, Pauline de. 1856. *Un regard écrit. Algérie*. Havre.

Pratt, Mary Louise. 1992. *Imperial Eyes: Travel Writing and Transculturation*. New York.

Reed, Christopher. 2017. *Bachelor Japanists: Japanese Aesthetics and Western Masculinities*. New York.

Sand, George. 1837. *Lettres d'un voyageur*. Paris.

Sims, Richard. 2001. *Japanese Political History Since the Meiji Restoration 1868–2000*. London.

Thompson, C. W. 2012. *French Romantic Travel Writing: Chateaubriand to Nerval*. Oxford.

Toussaint-Samson, Adèle. 1883. *Une Parisienne au Brésil*. Paris.

Ujfalvy-Bourdon, Marie de. 1880. *De Paris à Samarkand, Le Ferghanah, le Kouldja et la Sibérie orientale. Impressions d'une Parisienne*. Paris.

Yourcef, Abdeldjalil Larbi. 2020. "Pauline de Noirfontaine's *Un regard écrit: Algérie. Journal of Interdisciplinary History of Ideas* [Online] 18:1–9.

Chapter 7

Searching for a New Home, Losing the Self: The Birth and Death of Carlos Fuentes[1]

Roberta Micallef

In Iraq his name was Salim Abdul Husain, and.... He died in
Holland in 2009 under another name: Carlos Fuentes[2]

THE LAST OF A COLLECTION of fourteen short stories gathered in *The Corpse Exhibition* (2014) by Finland-based Iraqi author Hasan Blasim, "The Nightmares of Carlos Fuentes," recounts the story of a man who is part of the vast migration of peoples that started in the latter half of the twentieth century. In *Reflections on Exile* published in 2000, Edward Said wrote, "The greatest single fact of the past three decades has been, I believe, the vast human migration attendant upon war, colonialism and decolonization, economic and political revolution, and such devastating occurrences as famine, ethnic cleansing, and great power machinations."[3] "The Nightmares of Carlos Fuentes" starts and ends with images of physical death that haunt the protagonist's subconscious throughout the tale. Traveling from an unnamed city in Iraq to Amsterdam, Salim Abdul Husain masks his Arab identity and adopts a Mexican one because he believes that a non-Arab, brown identity will make it easier for him to assimilate.

In this tale, Blasim interrogates the notions of borders, identity, and belonging, as well as the concepts of home and being at home. The short story raises the issue of several types of borders: the body, national borders, cultural, social, and linguistic borders that parallel concepts of home. In this short story, the body is a home, the nation-state is a homeland, and the question of where the protagonist is at home or what he needs to do to be at home is the one that is raised but not answerable. In addition, this collection departs from traditional Middle Eastern diaspora narratives in several key ways. The oppressed intellectuals, the political asylum seekers, have been replaced by people from war-torn, violence-ridden, economically and environmentally devastated nation-states simply seeking bet-

---

1. I would like to thank James Uden, Mary Beth Raycraft, and Margaret Litvin for carefully reading and commenting on drafts of this essay.
2. Blasim 2014, 1.
3. Said 2000, XIV.

ter lives. Set in Amsterdam "The Nightmares of Carlos Fuentes" also decenters London and Paris as the geographic centers of the Arab diaspora in Europe. Twenty-first century Arab migration narratives such as Blasim's mark cities like Amsterdam, Stockholm, and Berlin as the sites of the new Arab diaspora.[4] Last but not least, this collection of short stories participates in destabilizing migration literature centered on binaries such as colonizer and colonized, as well as the conversation around passing, "a radical and transgressive practice that serves to destabilize and traverse the system of knowledge and vision upon which subjectivity and identity precariously rest."[5] Passing is an act that involves many participants who know the dominant narrative, a script that is already in existence. Those who are trying to pass are often challenging power structures and trying to play a part other than the one they were assigned by the accident of their birth.

Salim Abdul Husain first puts on a mask and tries to pass as someone that he is not, and then he tries to become Dutch. In his efforts to become Dutch, Salim Abdul Husain masters the language, gets a job, takes classes on Dutch culture and history, avoids getting into any legal trouble, and marries a Dutch woman. While he succeeds in becoming a Dutch citizen, he fails to become Dutch or eradicate his Iraqi identity. The prize for his efforts is not a life of peace and prosperity but rather death.

Here I examine the protagonist's strategies around masking and passing while traveling to make oneself at home in a new location. I examine topics that are relevant to all migration stories, and which are highlighted by this text: identity, belonging, and searching for a "home," where one can put down roots.

Crossing National Borders

When the readers are introduced to the protagonist, Salim Abdul Husain, on the first page of the story, he is already dreaming of crossing borders. A member of the municipality cleaning department, he is assigned to clear up after explosions. He and his colleagues are desensitized to the violence and destruction to the point that they are "bored and disgusted as every miserable day," they pick through the debris looking for human body parts.[6] He is consumed with thoughts of finding an intact wallet or such valuables that would allow him to buy a visa to Holland to escape this "hell of fire and death."[7] He finds a silver ring with an extraordinary gem that he transfers from the severed finger to his own and places the finger in a black plastic bag with other human body parts, and his adventure begins. The

---

4. Sellman 2018, 754.
5. Ahmed 1999, 88.
6. Blasim 2014, 187.
7. Blasim 2014, 187.

protagonist feels a secret spiritual connection to the ring and opts not to sell it.[8] Salim Abdul Husain's homeland is a hell full of death and destruction and the author introduces notions of loss of life and limbs as mundane and boring, even if disgusting. The body as the first "home" of its inhabitant, like this geographic homeland, is unable to protect or shelter its inhabitant.

The protagonist believes he can escape the violence and carnage of his homeland. Like many refugees, he believes that Europe is paradise. Similar to the refugees and asylum seekers whose stories populate Dina Nayeri's 2019 *The Ungrateful Refugee: What Immigrants Never Tell You,* he believes that if he can make it to Europe, he will be able to change the trajectory of his life. They believe "that if they can only be free of Iran, or Iraq or Turkey, life will be heaven,"[9] and so does he.

However, to make it into Europe he must first craft a story. In the *Ungrateful Refugee* Dina Nayeri tells her own story while investigating those of the "multitudes" seeking refuge in Greece and Holland. Based on her childhood experiences of refugee camps and those she has gathered as an adult researching refugees and refugee camps she emphasizes the importance of stories:

> In a refugee camp stories are everything....We had created our
> life's great story; next would come the waiting time, camp,
> where we would tell it. Then struggle for asylum, when we
> would craft it. Then assimilation into new lives, when we
> would perform it for the native-born, and finally, maybe in
> our old age, we would return to it, face it without frenzy: a
> repatriation.[10]

The border is a contact zone.[11] It is policed by officials charged with keeping out people like Salim Abdul Husain. He is not a true refugee. He has a job at home and no one is actively trying to kill him even if war and violence are always present. Power is distributed asymmetrically, and it is not on his side. However, like his foremother Scheherazade, he has the power of language and a storytelling tradition on his side.

Salim Abdul Husain is not particularly well educated, he has a middle school education. However, he is a cunning man who masters the art of autoethnography. He appropriates and uses the idioms of Europe to craft a story that is in dialogue with the stories circulating in the West about Islam, the Middle East, and even the United States.[12] He asks for a new name on the grounds that his

8. Blasim 2014, 188.
9. Nayeri 2019, 401–2.
10. Nayeri 2019, 36.
11. Pratt 1991, 34.
12. Pratt 1991, 35.

asylum request is based on his work for the US forces as a translator and he might be deemed a traitor to his country and be targeted for assassination by fanatical Islamist groups.[13] A fictitious story gets him through the border zone and out of the immigration center as well as a new name and identity, Carlos Fuentes. An Arab trying to pass as a Mexican may appear less transgressive in the world order of hegemonic identities than an Arab trying to pass as a white European. However, in that it reveals how a man simply trying to improve his lot in life by fleeing a homeland knows how to tell his story to gain entry to Europe and to seek acceptance it becomes the ultimate transgression. He is not a true refugee. If he were discovered he might be deemed an "opportunist," and sent back by those patrolling the border.

The story Salim Abdul Husain concocts intersects with news items appearing in conjunction with the initial US troop withdrawal from Iraq, which was completed in 2011. A National Public Radio news item aired on "Talk of the Nation" on January 4, 2012, is remarkably similar to Carlos Fuentes' story:

> For four years, an Iraqi named Tariq worked for the U.S. military as a translator. He's faced death threats from other Iraqis and asked to be identified by only his first name for his protection. Once the troops pulled out of the country, he lost his job and the on-base security that came with it.[14]

In the story of Salim Abdul Husain, the details the protagonist concocts are convincing enough that the Dutch officials let him into Holland, apparently unable or unwilling to check his credentials any further.

The path to Salim Abdul Husain becoming Carlos Fuentes deserves a closer examination because his rebirth takes place in a liminal space and requires a midwife. Salim calls his cousin from the immigration detention center, the ultimate liminal space, a no man's land between national spaces. His cousin inhaling pot while suppressing laughter tells him that he couldn't possibly have a European name like Jack or Stephen but that he should take a Cuban or Argentine name that would fit his complexion, which was "the color of burnt barley bread."[15] The same cousin suggests a literary name that he has stumbled upon in a newspaper article that he cannot understand but thought might be Spanish, Carlos Fuentes.[16] In the border zone in the immigration center, Salim Abdul Husain refashions himself and he is reborn with a new name, a new point of origin, a new socio-economic class background, and a fresh start to create new links to his

13. Blasim 2014, 188.
14. NPR 2012, https://www.npr.org/2012/01/04/144685821/uncertainty-for-iraqi-translator -after-withdrawal.
15. Blasim 2014, 188.
16. Blasim 2014, 188.

new society and to forge a new imagined community. In this act of transcultura-tion,[17] Salim Abdul Husain, a subaltern subject, selects and invents himself from materials transmitted from the culture section of a French newspaper, which was shared with him by his cousin, who is already established in France. While he is not putting on a literal mask, Salim constructs a new persona based on what he knows about Europeans.[18]

This renaming exercise adds some much needed levity to the topic of this short story. It is curious that the officials who granted him his wish by allow-ing his new name did not react to the name he chose for himself. Were they not aware of the Mexican writer and critic Carlos Fuentes? One might ask why Blasim chose to give Salim Abdul Husain this particular new name. Was it be-cause Carlos Fuentes was a rebel, wrote about national identity, and questioned society, or because his work was truly hybrid and included influences from many parts of the world? Or was it because Carlos Fuentes traveled throughout much of his life? It may have also been to demonstrate that even fame is fleeting. Or that those who can keep people out of national spaces are not particularly well educated.

The protagonist wastes no time creating a social and cultural mask of the person that he would like to be. Carlos begins to describe himself as "someone of Mexican origin whose father had left his country and settled in Iraq to work as an engineer with the oil companies."[19] Not only is he changing his national origin but he's also taking this opportunity to change his class position in society. Carlos Fuentes exhibits the same relationship to the idealized notion of "Holland" as the one described by Frantz Fanon in his 1950s psychological study of colonized Af-ricans and their relationship to France and whiteness. In *Black Skin White Masks* Fanon argues that Black Men want to be White, and in order to achieve this they learn the colonizer's language, for "a man who has a language consequently pos-sesses the world expressed and implied by that language."[20] Carlos Fuentes learns Dutch fluently, "in record time."

However, for Carlos Fuentes it was the Dutch girlfriend that was the pin-nacle of his effort to become integrated into Dutch society. In a light, cynical tone of writing Blasim pens some devastating lines: "The highlight of his efforts to integrate his mind and spirit into Dutch society came when he acquired a good-hearted Dutch girlfriend who loved and respected him. She weighed two hundred pounds and had childlike features, like a cartoon character. Fuentes

---

17. Pratt 1991, 36.

18. See Manuela Coppola's essay in this volume for a discussion of the process of inventing a new persona by imitating a culture that is largely imagined, in the context of eighteenth-century Jamaican creole society.

19. Blasim 2014, 190.

20. Fanon 1986, 18.

tried hard to treat her as a sensitive and liberated man would, like a Western man, in fact a little more so."[21]

That he "acquired" a Dutch girlfriend rather than found a partner or a friend is very much in line with his calculated, formulaic attempts at becoming Dutch. He doesn't realize that this is not a process that can take place beyond the border of his body. Travel is thought to transform a person. While the protagonist of this story is checking off a list of requirements to become the person he would like to become, the readers are not shown any evidence of a transformation. The fact that he "tried" to treat her as a Western man would tells us that he has not become a "sensitive and liberated" man. However, what is clear is that the protagonist is playing a part rather than being either Iraqi or Dutch.

It is not lost on the reader that this relationship and the female in the relationship is the opposite of the Eastern woman who is "acquired," by the Western colonizer and representatives. In *Imperial Fictions*, Rana Kabbani studies the production of the Eastern female as an exotic, erotic object of Western heterosexual male desires. Carlos Fuentes' wife is the opposite of the Oriental female as created in eighteenth and nineteenth-century Western art and travel literature. How are we to interpret the Dutch wife? Perhaps with a little help from Fanon. Fanon explains that for his colonized patients the love of a white woman was key to their entry and acceptance into French society:

> By loving me she proves that I am worthy of white love. I am
> loved like a white man. I am a white man. Her love takes me
> onto the noble road that leads to total realization.... I marry
> white culture, white beauty, white whiteness.[22]

Indeed, for Carlos Fuentes the highlight of his efforts is to integrate his mind and spirit into Dutch society, which tells us that he is having problems with both these aspects of his life. He believes that a girlfriend will be his guide into Dutch society. The contrast between the sexualized Eastern female prototype of the Western travel narratives studied by Kabbani and Carlos Fuentes' girlfriend further emphasizes the differences in their goals. The Western travelers represented colonizers; Carlos Fuentes is simply a man trying to change his life.

Carlos Fuentes exhibits some other traits that Nayeri documents in her research among refugees in Holland and Greece:

> And refugees arrive traumatized. Every last one, even the hap-
> piest, is broken in places.... Many suffer from shame, notions
> of inferiority. They are prone to embracing the very racism
> and classism that most harms them. They want to believe that

21. Blasim 2014, 190.
22. Blasim 2014, 63.

the systems are fair, that they can earn their way into the good
graces of the well-placed white man.[23]

Carlos Fuentes applies a particularly unforgiving gaze to his own people and
homeland. He has internalized racist attitudes towards the Arab world. He refus-
es to meet with Arabs or Iraqis because he has had "enough of misery, backwardness, death, shit, piss, and camels."[24] In the *Art of Seeing* John Berger describes the
effect of the male gaze on women. He writes,

> She has to survey everything she is and everything she does
> because how she appears to others, and ultimately how she
> appears to men, is of crucial importance for what is normally
> thought of as the success of her life. Her own sense of being in
> herself is supplanted by a sense of being appreciated as herself
> by another.[25]

Like women, Carlos Fuentes sees himself and his home through another's gaze.
Everything Carlos Fuentes sees "amazes and humiliates" him, including housing.
The word house connoting a physical, bounded space, another border, appears
three times in the story. The first two are a comparison between Iraqi houses and
Dutch ones: "We live in houses like pigsties while their houses are warm, safe,
and colorful."[26] And writing about immigrants and foreigners who are critical of
the Dutch, Carlos Fuentes thinks to himself: "They are Stone Age savages. They
hate the Dutch, who have fed and housed them."[27] In all three instances the emphasis is on the physical structure, how it looks, and cleanliness but there is no
information about the inhabitants of the Dutch houses while the immigrants are
likened to pigs and savages. Curiously neither the word nor the concept of home
is introduced anywhere in the story. While Arabic may not allow for a distinction
between home and house in the ways English does, Arab authors can and do
create images of homes that provide more than just shelter. The reader does not
read about Fuentes' home in Iraq and his dwelling in Holland is not described as
a home. He does not live in a space to which he has any emotional connection.

Carlos Fuentes behaves more Dutch than the Dutch themselves and is more
intolerant of fellow immigrants who don't follow the rules. He believes that with
every day that passes he is burying his past and his identity deeper. He commem-
orates the day he became a citizen and feels that even his body has changed.[28] For
the scholar of gender and sexuality studies Judith Butler, gender is an act that is

23. Nayeri 2019, 486.
24. Blasim 2014, 189.
25. Berger 2008, chapter 3.
26. Blasim 2014, 189.
27. Blasim 2014, 190.
28. Blasim 2014, 191.

well rehearsed that individuals are born into and that involves many players. For some, it is learned behavior that fits with social expectations and for some it is a type of passing, and for those who choose not to adhere to the roles they have been assigned it can be a cause of conflict. It is complicated by the fact that the play pre-exists the players and is a mediation between many actors and social as well as cultural expectations. The body becomes its gender "through a series of acts which are renewed, revised, and consolidated through time."[29] In this story, Salim Abdul Husain is wearing a social and cultural mask. He is willingly performing a part and while his body becomes its part, his subconscious does not cooperate. Carlos Fuentes feels that his skin and blood have changed, that his lungs function better now that this country respects him and that therefore he can worship it. That a citizen of a free and democratic state is not expected to worship his country is one of many subtle clues that Carlos Fuentes is going to face complications. Just as house or housing in this story never becomes a home or a place where the protagonist can be at home, while his body might have changed his mind is not at home in this new body. Despite appearances, Carlos Fuentes fails to reconcile his Iraqi identity with his newfound Mexican-via-Iraq European persona. He fails to go beyond being a Dutch citizen.

Carlos Fuentes does not appear to have emotional bonds with anyone including his wife. He doesn't mix with Arabs or Iraqis. He cannot mix with Spanish speakers. He is not a Mexican from Iraq. We have no sense that he is interacting with any Dutch people other than his wife and possibly his workmates. His physical body may have changed but he has not. That no one questions what it means to be a Mexican from Iraq and that no one attempts to speak to him in Spanish tells us how superficial his relationships are. In addition, the readers never see him interact with anyone. Passing successfully means that others believe who you claim to be. The text does not provide any evidence of successfully passing anywhere except in his own mind while he is awake. The lack of stories about his daily life, his interactions with people, and their reactions to him further emphasizes his isolation and loneliness.

Fanon's colonized patients want to become white in their dreams, and Fanon believes that, "[a]s a psychoanalyst, I should help my patient to become *conscious* of his unconscious and abandon his attempts at a hallucinatory whitening, but also to act in the direction of a change in the social structure."[30] The opposite is true for Carlos Fuentes. His motherland haunts his subconscious and won't let him forget who he really is.

> Motherlands are castles made of glass. In order to leave them,
> you have to break something – a wall, a social convention, a

29. Butler 1988.
30. Fanon 1986, 100.

cultural norm, a psychological barrier, a heart. What you have broken will haunt you. To be an émigré, therefore means to forever bear shards of glass in your pockets. It is easy to forget they are there, light and minuscule as they are, and go on with your life, your little ambitions and important plans, but at the slightest contact the shards will remind you of their presence. They will cut you deep.[31]

These shards show up in Carlos Fuentes' dreams. How his homeland and his native language appear in his dreams demonstrate what a tortured relationship he has to his homeland.

DREAMS AND TRAVEL

His daytime dreams of integration and assimilation turn into nightmares when he sleeps. In his sleep, Carlos Fuentes travels to his past, to his hometown. He has unpleasant encounters when he is reminded that he has not become Dutch and that he cannot escape his motherland or mother tongue. He is in particular haunted by the question of language. Carlos Fuentes argues that the Dutch government should send back refugees and immigrants who don't learn "the language properly."[32] The language that he thought was key to his acceptance in Holland, which he spent enormous amounts of time and energy mastering, is also a source of great anxiety for him. In his first disturbing dream, he sees himself unable to speak Dutch and speaking to his Dutch boss in an Iraqi Arabic dialect, which gives him a terrible headache.

Night after night his nightmares evolve and become more terrifying. In one, he is in the poor district in his hometown being chased by children who are making fun of him and verbalizing all his insecurities about his identity. Unlike his child-like bride, these children can see right through him. Unlike his wife, they are neither generous nor kind. They tease, they chase and they humiliate him. They call him a silly billy, a coward, and a sissy, not only assaulting his identity, but also his masculinity. Masculinity, like other aspects of identity, is constantly negotiated, created, and challenged in numerous ways.[33] If masculinity is a subjectivity linked to power created and propagated through various social forms,[34] in his new context his brand of masculinity is not hegemonic. Given that his first and most important conquest was the Dutch language, it seems natural that it would be the loss of language skills that would cause him the most anxiety.

31. Shafak 2020.
32. Blasim 2014, 190.
33. Reeser 2011, 18.
34. Reeser 2011, 21.

Indeed, in his dreams, first he loses his language skills. He is unable to speak Dutch or to communicate.[35] He has come to Holland to escape the violence of his homeland, the ever-present war. Yet in his dream he has brought the violence with him. He has brought a bomb to Amsterdam. In the following court case, the judges won't allow him to speak Dutch. This is humiliating. The translator can't understand his rustic accent. Here we see his carefully curated persona crumble. In his dream state, he seems to be wondering if the violence has not become part of him. Is that something he can actually get rid of? And when he uses his Iraqi dialect he reveals his class origins. He is no longer the son of a Mexican engineer. He is an Iraqi of lower socio-economic status. In his dreams, he is one of those refugees that he refers to as "retarded gerbils," or "stone-age savages."[36]

Carlos Fuentes works hard at finding a cure for his situation. He goes to the library and looks for books on dreams that might help free him from his nightmares. He comes across *The Forgotten Language*, a book by a widely read psychoanalyst, Eric Fromm.[37] Carlos Fuentes cannot understand much of Fromm's argument about the symbolic language of dreams. According to Fromm the language of symbol is "the one foreign language" we must all learn to understand ourselves, how we connect as human beings and what society chooses to repress. The readers see Carlos Fuentes quote and react to some of Fromm's ideas. Carlos Fuentes thinks that they are sheer nonsense:

> We are free when we are asleep, in fact freer than we are when
> awake.... We may resemble angels in that we are not subject
> to the laws of reality. During sleep the realm of necessity
> recedes and gives way to the realm of freedom. The existence
> of the ego becomes the only reference point for thoughts and
> feelings.[38]

Fuentes' middle school education and apparently all the coursework he did to familiarize himself with Dutch history and culture is not enough to allow him to comprehend Fromm's argument. Science and rational reasoning fail him. He continues to have problems communicating. While he clearly can use words, he cannot communicate his needs. He tries to explain what he needs to the librarian, who misunderstands him and suggests books about foods that help bring on peaceful sleep. As he fails to control his dreams and as they progressively become more nightmarish and he becomes more desperate to control his dreams, he tries more outlandish methods to deal with them. He stops eating root vegetables to

35. Blasim 2014, 191.
36. Blasim 2014, 190.
37. Blasim 2014, 192.
38. Blasim 2014, 192.

cut the symbolic connection with his roots. He stops going to bed naked and instead wears a thick coat because "nakedness attracts the reader to the zone of childhood."[39] Eventually his odd behavior causes strife with his wife. However, he can't share what is happening with her because that would be humiliating.[40] She is indulgent. She remembers how kind and generous he's always been. He now has to sleep on the couch in the living room. On one hand this darkly humorous passage serves as comic relief. However, it also paints Carlos Fuentes as a ridiculous, troubled man on the verge of a mental breakdown.

Carlos Fuentes convinces himself that if the dreams could only learn his new language, he would see new images when he slept. Finally, one of his wishes is granted when he becomes aware of the fact that he is dreaming in his own dream. In this terrible dream, he is back in Baghdad. He is perpetrating violence as his mask, Carlos Fuentes, when he comes face to face with Salim Abdul Husain.

> Salim was standing naked next to the window, holding a
> broom stained with blood. With a trembling hand Fuentes
> aimed his rifle at Salim's head. Salim began to smile and re-
> peated in derision, "Salim the Dutchman, Salim the Mexican,
> Salim the Iraqi, Salim the Frenchman, Salim the Indian,
> Salim the Pakistani, Salim the Nigerian ..."[41]

Ultimately, Carlos Fuentes sprays Salim with bullets, and Salim trying to escape jumps out a window and kills Carlos Fuentes and consequently himself. Edward Said, while reflecting on exile considers Simone Weil's question about the dilemma of exile. "To be rooted," she said, "is perhaps the most important and least recognized need of the human soul."[42] This dramatic encounter between Salim Abdul Husain and his alter ego Carlos Fuentes demonstrates his need "to be rooted," and the effect of severing his roots on his psyche.

This powerful and nightmarish scene highlights what is lost by the creation of the new persona who superficially appears to assimilate into a new homeland. The above lines speak to the anxiety about the loss of an identity that has not been replaced. Perhaps this is an anxiety the author, Hassan Blasim, shares with this fictional character he has brought into existence.

In an interview Blasim said:

> For years, the Iraqis were telling me: Your ideas are Western,
> go live in the West. And now the Finns have started saying:
> Go back to Iraq, quit talking about Finland. So where am

39. Blasim 2014, 194.
40. Blasim 2014, 194.
41. Blasim 2014, 195.
42. Weil quoted in Said 2000, 183.

I supposed to go? One newspaper asked me, "What's your country, your favorite country?" I was like: "My bed." It's the best place. I sleep there, I dream there. In fact I also eat in bed. I write. There's sex, there's everything. It's the best place …[43]

And yet the author's dilemma does not seem to be about performing one identity and endangering the "authentic" one. In the quote above the author seems to be refusing all imagined communities and refusing to try and mask and pass. Furthermore it appears that he also refused to mask and pass in Iraq. Perhaps he is suggesting that most people find themselves "masking" and "passing" to make it through daily life in any context.

While Blasim is referring to the way he is seen by those around him, Carlos Fuentes' struggles are entirely in his head or his subconscious. We never see what anyone else thinks of him or how they perceive him until his death. The next and final time Salim Abdul Husain's body crosses a physical border it is in a body bag. His story has been rewritten by the local media.

When Fuentes' wife woke up to the scream and stuck her head out the window, Carlos Fuentes was dead on the pavement, and a pool of blood was spreading slowly under his head. Perhaps Fuentes would have forgiven the Dutch newspapers, which wrote that an Iraqi man had committed suicide at night by jumping from a sixth-floor window, instead of writing that a Dutch national had committed suicide. But he will never forgive his brothers, who had his body taken back to Iraq and buried in the cemetery in Najaf.[44]

Upon his death, the story Salim Abdul Husain had written about himself, and that he worked hard to make real, was erased. The story written for him by the journalist is the one that became his for eternity. His mask was permanently removed. The accident of his birthplace became his defining characteristic. His Dutch era was obliterated and his body was taken back to Iraq by his biological family to rest for eternity. In a poignant circularity, he traveled home in a body bag like the one in which at the start of the story he was collecting body parts.

Like the circular nature of the opening scene and the closing scene of this short story, Salim Abdul Husain has returned to who he was at the beginning of the story. Quite literally his true self has murdered his made-up persona and thereby removed his carefully constructed mask. Fanon writes that every colonized people – in other words, every people in whose soul an inferiority complex

43. Litvin and Sellman, 2016.
44. Blasim 2014, 195–196.

has been created by the death and burial of its local cultural originality – finds itself face to face with the language of the civilizing nation; that is, with the culture of the mother country. The colonized is elevated above his jungle status in proportion to his adoption of the mother country's cultural standards.[45] When trying to transform himself into Carlos Fuentes, Salim certainly demonstrated that he had internalized these thoughts. He thought poorly of his countrymen and his country. He believed that he could rise above the other refugees and asylum seekers. Fanon suggests that the solution is in liberating the man of color from himself.[46] Carlos Fuentes fails completely in liberating himself from himself and his own prejudices about his own country and people like him. Rather than figuring out who he is and how to be human and how to find common ground with others, he takes on a name whose historical weight and significance he doesn't understand. He looks for solutions to his problems in books he cannot understand. Instead of truly familiarizing himself with a language, any language that would allow him to gain knowledge about himself and what makes him human, he puts on a mask and looks for solutions in repetitive behaviors to allow him to become what he wants to be most, Dutch.

This text is as interesting in what it leaves unsaid as it is in what it says. In Holland, we never hear about his encounters with the Dutch apart, from his wife. Indeed the reader is left with the sense that Carlos Fuentes remains a stranger to Dutch society. He may be part of the workforce, live there, and even be a citizen. However, socially he remains a stranger to everyone including his wife. Apart from one mention of his boss in a dream, there is no evidence of any interaction with Dutch society. It appears that the only one convinced by his masking and the only one for whom he managed to pass was himself. If all our identity is an ever-fluctuating negotiation with those around us, a play in which we act and are judged on how well we play our part, even though he checked all the boxes and repeatedly played the same role there is no evidence that he understood the play or was even "passing" credibly. Whom has this man actually fooled?

One might say that Salim Abdul Husain has a homeland but his homeland is a hellscape. And his body, the shell that contains him becomes uninhabitable. He is unable to rest or find any peace in his body. In Holland, he becomes a citizen but he never becomes rooted. While both Salim Abdul Husain and Carlos Fuentes inhabit physical spaces that are homes they are never "at home."

Neither immigrant we meet in this story, Salih Abdul Husain nor his unnamed cousin in France, know the languages of their new homelands well enough to understand symbolic or abstract language. They can glean facts such

45. Fanon 1986, 18.
46. Fanon 1986, 10.

as the name of an author but nothing beyond that. They are not connected to the culture or arts of their new homelands. Salih Abdul Husain knows who he does not want to be. Carlos Fuentes does not know who he is. Salih Abdul Husain's attempts at masking and passing are a failure because he wanted the mask to become permanent without either accepting himself for who he was or learning from his experiences and transforming. Our protagonist simply tries to erase his past in its entirety, which leads him to become completely unmoored and at war with himself, which eventually leads to his death.

In his interview with Litvin and Sellman, Blasim suggests that the solution to identity problems and survival in the modern world is diversity in thought, culture, art, and being connected and hybridity.[47]

> [A]nd you're part of the world. Of the Earth, the planet. You're part of it all. It's all linked. But then people start talking about being pure, just this or that, like, "You're Finnish," or "You're Iraqi," or "You're an engineer," and nothing else. That's so limited. You're everything. You're an engineer, an artist, a dead person, you're nothingness, you're a dream. This connectedness it helps you write better. If you're limited, you'll think in a limited way. And that's our problem in the Arab world. People don't accept diversity. You just have to be Arab, Muslim. Our ancient literature was beautiful, with the interpenetration of civilizations, we discarded this and focused on religion. What I mean is, this interpenetration and connectedness is part of who I am now, the way I think. [48]

Salim Abdul Husain and Carlos Fuentes are lacking in connectivity. If what makes us human is our ability to use abstract, symbolic language, to create art, and to learn from and be inspired by other humans whether from the 1001 Nights or the art of Van Gogh, Carlos Fuentes dies because while focusing on becoming a Dutch citizen he has neglected to learn about himself. With this quote above Blasim allows us to read "The Nightmares of Carlos Fuentes" ironically. He rescues us from being stuck in the binary of "us vs. them," "colonizer vs. colonized," "refugee vs. national," or more specifically, "Iraqi vs. Dutch." The quote allows us to think about belonging and identity as multi-layered garments that we can choose to layer differently to allow us to live comfortably in our social and cultural milieu, and to discard when needed so that we can simply meet each other as human beings rather than representatives of different imagined communities.

47. Litvin and Sellman 2016.
48. Litvin and Sellman 2016.

Bibliography

Ahmed, Sarah. 1999. "She'll Wake Up One of These Days and Find That She's Turned into a Nigger Passing through Hybridity." *Theory, Culture and Society* 16 (2): 87–106. ISSN 0263-2764.

Berger, John. 2008. *Ways of Seeing*. London. First published in 1972.

Blasim, Hassan. 2014. *The Corpse Exhibition and Other Stories of Iraq*. Translated by Jonathan Wright. New York.

Butler, Judith. 1988. "Performative Acts and Gender Constitution: An Essay in Phenomenology and Feminist Theory." https://guttmancuny.digication. com/humanities_foundations_mead/Butler.

Fanon, Frantz and Charles L. Markmann. 1986. *Black Skins White Masks: The Experiences of a Black Man in a White World*. New York.

The Foreigner's Home. 2018. Directors Rian Brown and Geoff Pingree. An exploration of Toni Morrison's artistic vision based on a series of 2006 lectures delivered at the Louvre and interactions with artists. A French-American co-production.

Guenther, Sebastian and Stephan Milich, eds. 2016. "Introduction" *Representations and Visions of Homeland in Modern Arabic Literature*. Zurich and New York.

Kabbani, Rana. 2008. *Imperial Fictions: Europe's Myths of the Orient*. London.

Litvin, Margaret, and Johanna Sellman. 2016. Hassan Blasim Interview. *Tank*, August 2016. https://tankmagazine.com/issue-69/talk/hassan-blasim.

Marchi, Lisa. 2014. "Ghosts, Guests, Hosts: Rethinking 'Illegal' Migration and Hospitality Through Arab Diasporic Literature." *Comparative Literature Studies* 51 (4): 603–26. *JSTOR*, https://doi.org/10.5325/ complitstudies.51.4.0603.

Marandi, S. M., and E. Shabanirad. (2015). "Edward Said's Orientalism and the Representation of Oriental Women in George Orwell's *Burmese Days*. *International Letters of Social and Humanistic Sciences* 60:22–33. https:// doi.org/10.18052/www.scipress.com/ILSHS.60.22.

Nayeri, Dina. 2019. *The Ungrateful Refugee: What Immigrants Never Tell You*. New York.

Nostrand, Richard L., and Lawrence E. Estaville Jr. 1993. "Introduction: The Homeland Concept." *Journal of Cultural Geography* 13 (2): 1–4. DOI: 10.1080/08873639309478384.

Pratt, Mary Louise. 1991. "Arts of the Contact Zone." *Profession*: 33–40. *JSTOR*, http://www.jstor.org/stable/25595469.

Reeser, Todd W. 2011. *Masculinities in Theory: An Introduction*. http://public. eblib.com/choice/publicfullrecord.aspx?p=819404.

Said, Edward. 2000. *Reflections on Exile and Other Essays*. Cambridge.

Sellman, Johanna. 2018. "A Global Postcolonial: Contemporary Arabic Literature of Migration to Europe." *Journal of Postcolonial Writing* 54 (6): 751–65. DOI: 10.1080/17449855.2018.1555207

Shafak Elif. 2020. "On What it Means to Belong in Many Places at Once." *Literary Hub.* https://lithub.com/elif-shafak-on-what-it-means-to-belong-in-many-places-at-once/

Williams, Patrick, and Laura Chrisman. 2015. *Colonial Discourse and Post-Colonial Theory: A Reader.* ProQuest Ebook Central. http://ebookcentral.proquest.com/lib/bu/detail.action?docID=3570344.

Chapter 8

A Role to Be Negotiated:
Mei Lanfang's Visit to the USSR (1935)

Catherine Yeh

Figure 1. Picture taken when Sergei Eisenstein directed and filmed a few scenes from Mei Lanfang performing "Rainbow Pass." Mei Lanfang, dressed in traditional Peking opera costume in the role of Lady Dongfang, with Eisenstein (first row, second from left), Yu Shangyuan (top row, left), Sergei Tretyakov (top row, middle), Zhang Pengchun (Chang Peng-chun; top row, right), and other Soviet dramatists. 1935. Source: Mei Shaowu 1997, 203.

AT THE INVITATION of the All-Union Society for Cultural Relationships with Foreign Countries (VOKS), Mei Lanfang traveled to the USSR and performed in Moscow and Leningrad in March and April of 1935. The program included "The Beauty Defies Tyranny," "The Fisherman's Revenge," "Rainbow Pass," "The Drunken Beauty," "By Phin River Bend," "Fooling the Tiger General," together with several dance parts of other plays. Mei's performances won warm applause and his performing art was highly praised by Konstantin

Stanislavsky, Nemirovich-Danchenko, W. E, Meyerhold, S. M. Eisenstein, and the German dramatists Erwin Piscator and Bertolt Brecht. Following in the footsteps of Mei's America visit in 1930, the visit to the USSR firmly established Mei as an international performing artist and star.

Scholarship regarding this visit to the USSR by Mei Lanfang has largely focused on the reception of Mei's art by artists working in the former Soviet Union and other European theater artists, including Bertolt Brecht.[1] These studies share the basic assumption that Chinese art is being consumed by the Soviet avant-garde based on their own needs and preoccupations, and that these artists judged Chinese theater art through their own cultural lens. There is also the notion that Peking opera was being misrepresented through conceptual mislabeling. Some even go so far as to accuse the Soviet artists of "appropriating" Chinese theater aesthetics.[2]

The question we might ask is whether culture migration necessarily entails some degree of "misreading," "misunderstanding," and "misinterpretation"? Might it not be that this process embodies the very nature of transcultural interaction? A case can be made that as migration takes place, one set of cultural "vocabulary" and "grammar" based on an array of assumptions and cultural traditions is transmitted and given a local identity as it enters into a different cultural structure. In most cases, for this knowledge to have any local significance, it must be made relevant on local terms. In an essential way the process necessarily entails a form of "masking," both on the transmitting side and on the receiving side. To be accepted by local culture both sides mask the identity of this new import and attempt to interpret and integrate it into the local cultural structure. By branding Peking opera as "symbolic art," Western artists and critics were able to comprehend and accept Peking opera aesthetics. In turn, this branding was accepted by Mei Lanfang, who willingly offered it as a conceptual framework to situate Peking opera in world theater aesthetics. Thus, in the transmission process, "misrepresentation," "mispresentation," and "mistranslation," are forms of cultural camouflage. It is an essential part of integrating new knowledge coming from outside. In the case of Mei Lanfang, by traveling from China to Russia and through his actual performance, a very real form of communication between two quite disparate cultural structures became both possible and mutually beneficial. The excitement it generated among the Soviet artists was due to a sense of the totally alien nature of the art of Peking opera, and as such it was without any social connotations and cultural associations. The lack of cultural reference points stimulated the imagination of Soviet avant-garde artists, and understanding was achieved necessarily through the local reception of the new information. The

1. Saiussy 2006, 8–29.
2. Min Tian 2012, 14.

Russians thus understood Peking opera as "symbolic art" using Eisenstein's term, the art of "imagery."[3]

Cultural migration takes place through the act of "translations." The photograph which opens this paper shows that this new cultural import brought by Mei Lanfang's visit to the USSR was framed as authentic Chinese culture: Mei Lanfang in his persona as female impersonator and actor reinforces this sense of authenticity and at the same time by sitting among the Soviet artists reinforces its local identify in a global setting.

Within this framework of cultural migration, and to further the discussion on the concept of "masking" or "misdirection" as part of the normal process of localization of global cultural trends, in this study I will analyze the dynamic interaction between Mei Lanfang's projection of traditional Chinese culture and its reception by the Soviet artists in Moscow in 1935. This will involve examining the program Mei Lanfang presented during his tour, the process of filming of Mei Lanfang's performance of "Rainbow Pass" by Eisenstein, and the cultural exchanges that took place during Mei's visit that led to both the Soviets and Mei to understand the significance of traditional Chinese opera within a global context. Culture migrates in response to a local pull. Both Mei Lanfang and the Soviet artists were faced with very concrete challenges rather different in nature. This study will situate Mei's visit within this historical context.

To establish the historical and cultural context for this case study, we will need to deal with Mei Lanfang's motivation in accepting the Soviet invitation. By traveling and performing in Russia in person, what did Mei want to achieve? What was the significance as well as social standing of traditional folk culture as represented by Peking opera for the modernist artist in the Soviet Union as well at the time? Mei Lanfang's visit took place one year after the 1934 Soviet Writers' Congress, where the doctrine of socialist realism was officially codified. Representing the quintessential old cultural order, Mei Lanfang as a male actor playing the female role known as *dan*, both aesthetically as well as ideologically, seem to stand at the other end of the spectrum to socialist realism. Instead of the new opera created by Mei Lanfang and his supporters that are closer to contemporary life and the struggles of women, the operas chosen by the VOKS and the Soviet dramatists all appear to belong to the traditional repertoire. How did Mei Lanfang's artistic style serve the needs of socialist realism or socialist society? And how did Mei himself understand his mission to the Soviet Union?

SOCIALIST REALISM VERSUS SYMBOLIC ABSTRACT ART

From the photograph at the beginning of this study (Figure 1), it is clear that Mei Lanfang is playing a part; he is seen in theatrical costume, a male actor in

---

3. Eisenstein 1935, 769.

masque posing as a female. From the dynamics shown in the photo featuring Mei Lanfang and famous Soviet filmmakers and dramatists, some clues are made visible. It is not a coincidence that Mei Lanfang is shown wearing his Peking opera costume. Traditional Chinese folk culture is staged in the photo for a reason. It stands in contrast to both Western realism and socialist realism. Seen in its isolated and minority status, it is presented as nonthreatening. In Mei Lanfang's posture, there is a sense of calm acceptance of him playing the role of a representative of an exotic tradition.

His attitude reflects his success in transmitting the principle governing Peking opera aesthetics to his Soviet host and that its system was regarded as the highest expression of art. According to Eisenstein, "In its own sphere [Peking opera] is the acme of perfection, the sum total of those elements that form the kernel of any art work – its imagery."[4] After seeing Mei perform and through their discussions with Mei Lanfang on Peking opera aesthetics, Soviet avant-garde artists understood Peking opera as representing the fruition of a long historical tradition. As they saw it, Chinese theater had reached maturity in the twelfth century, and they were convinced that it still had a role to play in providing socialist realism with much needed artistic inspiration and formal ingredients. Eisenstein was convinced that the experience to be derived from the Chinese theater was even wider and deeper than that of the impact of Japanese Kabuki theater had had on Soviet sound cinema.[5] He further spelled out the dynamic relationship between traditional art versus the newly forming socialist realism:

> The problem of imagery is one of the main problems of our new [socialist realism] aesthetics. While we are fast learning to develop our characters psychologically, we still lack a great deal when it comes to imagery. And here we come upon the most interesting aspect of Chinese culture – the theatre. Imagery in Chinese art is emphasized at the expense of the concrete and the thematic. This emphasis is the antithesis of the hypertrophy of imagery upon which our art is still based. Is the polarity of these two approaches incompatible? Not at all. They are just two extremes in the development of those traits which, when they will blend into one harmonious whole, will give the highest phase of realism.[6]

Eisenstein's response to Mei Lanfang's performance is a clear illustration of the dynamics of transcultural interaction. He recognized the shortcoming and inadequacy of socialist realism and viewed Peking opera's aesthetics from this point

4. Eisenstein 1935, 769.
5. Eisenstein 1935, 769.
6. Eisenstein 1935, 769–70.

of view of lack. As pointed out by Haun Saussy in his excellent study of Mei
Lanfang's visit to the USSR, different artists saw in Mei Lanfang's art something
they felt was important in addressing the shortcomings of different aspects of
realism.[7] In the photograph (Figure 1) then, Mei Lanfang stands for a pure form
of symbolic art consisting of imageries distilled from the past; and as an aesthetic
form it stands opposite to realism. As Eisenstein sees it, the aesthetics of Peking
opera excels because it is free from "the concrete and the thematic [realism]."[8]

REALISM VERSUS OLD FEUDAL TRADITIONAL: THE CHINESE SCENARIO

While Peking opera as a Chinese traditional art form was being lauded by the
Soviet modernist artists, in China it had been the target of much criticism from
the Chinese political reformers since late nineteenth century. This criticism in-
tensified after the 1911 Republican revolution and during the 1919 May Fourth
new cultural movement. The main criticism from the radical cultural elite was
that Peking opera represented old China, and the traditional cultural values of
its feudal past. The critique largely comes from Western-educated youth who regarded Western realistic aesthetic as the highest register of theater art.[9] They tried
to introduce Western-style realistic spoken drama to the Chinese stage and wanted to eliminate traditional Chinese theater art. Although Peking opera continued
to be loved by Chinese audiences throughout the early decades of the twentieth
century and was supported by reform-minded playwrights, nonetheless, its leading role on the Chinese stage, and its relevance for modern Chinese society was
called into question.

Mei Lanfang and Peking opera supporters recognized the danger this challenge posed to Peking opera in the long run. They set out to prove that this traditional art form had the potential to inspire reform and renovation, and continued
to have great relevance for modern times. They argued that Peking opera did not
necessarily represent only the past, as the May Fourth youth seem to believe, but
that it had a future in helping to modernize China. Mei Lanfang was committed
to forging a path that singled Peking opera modernity.[10] At first, he experimented
with realism, but this was quickly abandoned. Being understood by foreign audience and critiques as representing an art form from ancient times, Mei and his
supporters realized that realism was not the solution for Peking opera's survival.
The solution was to be found in creating new aesthetic forms that both repre-

---

7. Saussy 1935, 8–29.
8. Eisenstein 1935, 769
9. Goldstein 2007, 134–171.
10. For an in-depth discussion on the Peking opera reform and the historical debate on realism
relating to Mei Lanfang's visit to the Soviet Union in 1935, see Jiang, Ji. 2022.

sented modernity and had roots in Peking opera tradition. This was achieved through reviving the long forgotten dance tradition that once was prevalent in southern Chinese opera.[11] During the 1910s, with the rise of modern dance in Europe and America, dance was understood by Mei Lanfang and his supporter as representing modernity. Accordingly, Mei Lanfang experimented with recreating and reinserting traditional Chinese dance into Peking opera. Dance drama thus became the signature of Mei Lanfang's performance, and the (re)introduction of dance became the main structural transformation that reshaped Peking opera in the 1910s and 20s.[12]

To secure Peking opera's standing in modern China, gaining global recognition and acceptance was seen as crucial. Dance was understood as a universal language. It's insertion into Peking opera was motivated by the need to gain international audience acceptance and appreciation. Thus, while continuing to reform Peking opera by producing up-to-date socially informed new operas, the transformation of Peking opera aesthetics by introducing the newly invented traditional dance was seen by Mei Lanfang and his supporters as a key strategy for gaining Western audiences and Western cultural elites' approval and support.

This was achieved through exposing foreign audiences to this new form of art through performances to foreigners who had traveled to China and through foreign travels by Mei Lanfang. As he had become the most famous Peking opera star, Mei actively engaged with foreign visitors to China and performed for them. This helped spread his fame abroad. Then came the foreign visits, first to Japan in 1919, then to the United States in 1930, and finally to the USSR in 1935. With each tour, Mei Lanfang increasingly understood that the future Peking opera's role within the global modern theater setting lay in representing traditional Chinese theater.

The reform of Peking opera was the result of transcultural engagement and actively joining the global theater aesthetics exchanges. These foreign visits and the acceptance of Peking opera by prominent foreign artists helped secure its position in China, and they also helped Mei Lanfang revise his understanding of Peking opera reform. It encouraged Mei and his supporters to abandon their original idea of reforming Peking opera to make it more realistic. After each visit, Mei and his supporters found new theatrical support for Peking opera's modern value. After the visit to Japan, from the positive responses of audience and critics to his new dance dramas, Mei became convinced that to gain international recognition, Peking opera had to be engaged with contemporary issues concerning social progress. After the visit to the United Sates, Mei and his clique decided that Peking opera should represent symbolic art. The most lauded US performances were dynamic dance dramas with dramatic plots. And through the visit to the

11. Yeh 2016, 28–37.
12. Yeh 2020, 44–59.

USSR, Mei Lanfang hoped to further gain recognition and promote the significance of Peking opera aesthetic as contributing to the modernist movement.

THE PROGRAM WAS TAILOR-MADE FOR SOVIET RUSSIA

From Mei's performance program in the USSR, it is clear that the Soviet cultural authorities and Mei Lanfang's delegation devised a program that suited both the ideological needs of the Soviet Union and Mei Lanfang's delegation's desire to impress the Soviet audience and provide Soviet theater critics with a type of drama that they would be able to appreciate. Compared to the programs Mei performed in Japan and the United States, special consideration was given to local reception.[13] Highly aware of the potential significance of his visit to the leading socialist nation, Mei Lanfang adjusted his performance to fit the cultural polities of the Soviet Union at the time. His program highlighted the rebelliousness and resilience of the female character. In terms of formal aspects, as in Japan and United States, the program in the Soviet Union focused largely on dance dramas. In the USSR, however, the dance dramas highlighted both martial arts (dancing with

Figure 2. The sword dance performance by Mei Lanfang at a reception party in Moscow, 1935. Source: Mei Shaowu 1997.

13. For a comparative study of the programs performed by Mei Lanfang in Japan (1919), USA (1930) and the USSR (1935) see Yeh 2007.

Figure 3. Mei Lanfang as Xiao Guiying in "The Fisherman's Revenge," performed in Moscow, 1935. Source: Mei Shaowu 1997.

different forms of weapons) and dramas featuring the heroine wielding a weapon, featuring multiple performances of the sword dance and the spear dance.[14]

The dancing female wielding different types of weapons clearly demonstrates female agency in these dramas. The weapons become the extension and outer expression of the heroine's spirit and her determination to fight for justice. Yet,

14. Program illustrations from these performances may be found in Performances 1935.

these dance dramas are largely new creations inserted into existing operas, and transforming them. They seem traditional, but they are new in their ideological orientatation and in their aesthetic forms. The central figures of the rebellious heroine, the female warrior, and the unyielding wife, daughter, and women warrior are entirely twentieth-century creations.

This image was reinforced by the program designed for the Soviets. To suit the Soviet audiences and theater critics, most of the operas performed in the Soviet Union underwent adjustments. The aim of these adjustments was to rid them of any sign of what might be perceived as "backwardness" and might be deemed as incompatible with modern Western civilized standards or representing the feudal social structure and relationships. This included restaging and reinterpreting the plays and their main heroine. One example is the opera "Yuzhou feng" [The Precious Sword Named], also translated as "Madness by Pretense"), in which Mei Lanfang played the heroine Zhao Yanrong (Figure 4).

Figure 4. Mei Lanfang in "Yuzhou Feng" [The Precious Sword named Yuzhou Feng]. Photograph. Source: A. C. Scott, *Mei Lan0fang Leader of the Pear Garden*. Hong Kong: Hong Kong University Press, 1959. p. 72.

The original opera focused on the struggle between two ministers in the court of the Second Qin Emperor (210–207 BCE). In Mei Lanfang's new opera, he takes one scene from this male-dominated drama and turns it into a female-centered story. It featured Zhao Yanrong, as the virtuous daughter of one of the ministers, and re-interprets the play as a story of rebellion where the heroine goes against the will of both her father and the emperor. In the opera "A Nun Seeks Love" (Si fan), Mei Lanfang choreographed a dance for the character of the teenage nun. This again was a famous traditional play. It focused on the sexual awakening of young women and traditionally was known for its rather explicit sexual allusions and innuendos. It was a play that was banned at different periods in China due to it lewdness. Mei Lanfang's performance of it reinterpreted the desires of the young women as a legitimate yearning for love, thus attempting to reshape the sentiments of the heroine to make them more compatible with the modern Western ideal of the individual rights to free love. To further emphasize the justice of the deadly struggle the women are involved in, some plays were renamed to highlight this point. The play "Dayu shajia" was originally translated as "The Fisherman's Revenge" in the program performed in the United States. For the Soviet performance, it was translated instead as "The Revenge of the Oppressed." The program was selected and presented in Soviet Russia with new choreography, a rewritten script, and a reinterpretation of characters, all aimed at highlighting Peking opera's modernity. Reshaping the female characters fit the requirements of socialist ideology that drama should represent the struggles of the people against oppression.

The Dance Drama "Rainbow Pass" Framed within Peking Opera Tradition and its Cultural Migration through Film

During Mei Lanfang's visit, Eisenstein made a short film based on a few scenes from "Rainbow Pass." Thanks to this short film sequence, "Rainbow Pass" has become the most famous record available to us today of Mei Lanfang's performances in Russia in 1935.

The photo was taken at the time of the shooting of the film. In this photo, we see Mei Lanfang performing the role of Lady Dongfang (the dancing figure on the left raising a sword), with Eisenstein mimicking Mei's hand and body gestures. The process by which Mei Lanfang's performance transitioned from stage art to film art captured a complex cultural moment. The filming of the opera shows the process of marrying a local art form, namely Peking opera, with a global technologically driven art form, namely film.

The story of "The Rainbow Pass" features the government army waging a battle to capture the breakaway town of Hongniguan. The defender, Xin Wenli,

Figure 5. S. M. Eisenstein directed and filmed a few scenes from Mei's "Rainbow Pass." Mei Lanfang playing the role of Lady Dongfang is on the left, Eisenstein stands in the back, between Mei Lanfang and the actor playing the role of Wang Bodang on the right. Source: Mei Shaowu 1997, 202.

refused to fight, and was shot to death by the warrior Wang Bodang. Xin Wenli's wife, Lady Dongfang was a renowned beauty and a warrior in her own right who took to arms to revenge her husband's death. When Lady Dongfang and Wang Bodang came face to face on the battlefield, they were paralyzed by the longing they felt for each other and were unable to fight. Lady Dongfang managed in the end to capture Wang Bodang. Because she admired the handsome Wang Bodang, she agreed to his demand to surrender the town to the government forces while he in turn surrendered himself to her and became her new husband. In Mei Lanfang's reinterpretation, the heroine Lady Dongfang becomes a psychologically complex character. Representing modern values, his interpretation of the story emphasizes female agency, self-determination, and free love.

According to Mei Lanfang, Eisenstein discussed the making of a short film on Mei's performance for the larger Soviet public that was aware of Mei's visit and performance through the news media, but was unable to see him in the theater. Eisenstein's film is a short take on the scene between Lady Dongfang and Wang Bodang when they finally set eyes on each another on the battlefield and fall in love. According to Mei Lanfang, he suggested to Eisenstein that the dance movements should be filmed with "both actors shot together, otherwise it will appear dull and disconnected." Mei further suggested the best way to achieve this was to use more medium longshots and longshots, and fewer close-ups and medium close-ups. According to Mei Lanfang, "In this manner, it might be easier to display the characteristics of Chinese opera." What Mei emphasized is the pas de deux nature of the battle-dance. Eisenstein agreed in principle, however, he added, "But close-ups must be woven in because, as you know, Soviet audiences crave to see your face!"

These two approaches towards filming the fighting scene reflect two different artistic orientations. In the art of Peking opera, the emphasis is on the duality of male and female interaction, known as the *sheng* (生) and *dan* (旦) interaction that forms the basic plot structure. In Western cinematography, the star-led plot structure called for the use of close-ups to identify as well as understand the inner workings of the hero or heroine. Mei Lanfang's suggestion to use medium long-shots and longshots reflects traditional Peking opera aesthetics. Yet, most of his newly created operas were all female-centered plays, with him as the star. Mei's performances were also highly psychological. He expressed the inner feelings of characters not only through traditional formal gestures, but influenced by photography and motion pictures. Mei made extensive use of his eyes and facial expressions to convey the inner emotions of the characters he portrayed. Eisenstein saw this in Mei's acting and intuitively understood its filming possibilities. For Mei Lanfang's performance, star-focused filming techniques and closeups were eminently suitable. He also knew very well the power of the close shot within the film medium and the audience's expectations and anticipations. Yet, Eisenstein did not insert closeups in this short film.[15]

The filming proved to be a difficult process and took many hours. There were many takes, and Eisenstein was constantly dissatisfied with the results. He wanted to be able to film the whole sequence in one take, but repeatedly mistakes were made and each time the scene had to be filmed again from the beginning. Furthermore, Eisenstein was concerned with where to cut the scene so as to be able to insert the close ups on Mei's face. Again, Eisenstein and Mei Lanfang discussed in detail the plot and the lyrics of the scene and where the cut/break might take place. Eisenstein's ideal outcome for the film was to "aim both at preserving a sense of artistic totality [of the scene/the art of Peking opera]" and at the same time "letting [Mei's] face standout."[16]

As this was a film with sound, there was also the issue of the live music

15. Eisenstein's Film with Mei Lanfang performing (1935). https://www.youtube.com/watch?v=4nlf5LW_nrQ

16. Mei Lanfang 1962, 40–49, and translation by Rebull 2010.

played by Chinese musicians with traditional Chinese instruments. The microphones were hanging in midair, but the vibration from the instruments varied from high to low and loud to soft, so the position of the orchestra couldn't be the same as when performing onstage, where they could all be gathered together. Some of the traditional instruments, for example the drum and the large gong, had to be stationed further away, but the *huqin* had to be a little closer as its sounds was light in comparison.

According to Mei Lanfang, the filming process forced the actors into a relatively passive position. The end product suggests that Eisenstein attempted to realize his understanding of the aesthetic of Peking opera as an art of imageries at the "expense of the concrete and the thematic."[17] Eisenstein attempted to capture the fighting scene using the long shot. For the psychologically charged scenes where Lady Dongfang and Wang Bodang confront one another, he used the medium shot. Through the long and medium closeups shots he tried to bring about what he considered the highest form of art – a blend of psychological realism and imagery-based symbolism – into one harmonious whole.[18] The medium closeup served as the formal link between the two forms of art. The result was a successful hybrid product that combined film and stage art.

The film centered on presenting Chinese opera with all its different dimensions, including dancing, singing, and acting. Because of his agenda, Eisenstein sacrificed his desire to use close-ups on Mei's face. At the same time, he was also not interested in reproducing the dynamism of the martial fighting scene by adjusting it to the editing process of film art. In other words, he was not interested in reproducing stage art. Rather, he experimented with uniting film art with theater art. This might explain why a seasoned filmmaker like Eisenstein did not move the camera from a frontal position facing the action. The only movement was to shorten the distance. Thus, the fighting scene appeared static. The usage of different shot angles would have offered possibilities for editing and would have strengthened the film. But that was not Eisenstein's objective. As he stated, he desired to preserve the integrity and unity of Peking opera aesthetics. As a result, he needed to redirect the filming technique from its establish grammar to a transcultural and trans-genre end point. The only psychological study of the characters came when he used the medium closeup. This is because he wanted to capture the pivotal moment of Lady Dongfang's transformation from fighting with hatred in order to avenge the death of her husband, to falling in love with the enemy on the battlefield. This was also the moment where the blending of film art and Chinese theater art was realized.

17. Eisenstein 1935, 769.
18. Eisensteain 1935, 769.

CONCLUSION

Mei Lanfang's visit to the USSR can be regarded as a landmark moment in trans-cultural interaction. It helped further Chinese theater's joining the international modernist discussion. As in all transcultural exchanges, the attempt to be under-stood engendered greater self- understanding and clarity about one's own needs. The desire to be understood lead to formal adjustments. In this case, the insertion of dances into Peking opera as a transcultural form of aesthetic communication also gave Peking opera its modern signature. To meet the expectation of the au-dience of a socialist country where class and class struggle and the liberation of the oppressed people were its dominant ideology, Mei Lanfang readjusted and reinterpreted existing Peking opera programs. The act of reinterpretation can be considered as the necessary "masking" in the process of transcultural exchange But this masking, while originally made for the immediate purpose of winning acceptance by Soviet audiences and critics, would have a long lasting impact on Mei Lanfang's performance. By centering the women figure on stage and accen-tuating her rebellious and fighting spirit, Mei Lanfang helped usher Peking opera into the modern period. For the Soviets, the excitement brought about by Mei's performance simulated creativity and self-critique among the Soviet artists, as reflected by Eisenstein's discussion of Chinese theater and of his filming of "The Rainbow Pass."

The timing of the visit was also important for both sides. Mei Lanfang's jour-ney to the Soviet Union came at a delicate moment in history. Up to that time, Western art, literature, and drama had been largely based on realism. However, many artists felt that realism had exhausted its possibilities and fatigue was setting in. Western dramatists were searching for new sources of stimulation to break through realism's limits. At the same time, Mei Lanfang's experimental Peking opera, in which he had introduced dance since the 1910s, challenged realism's aesthetic values. For Mei Lanfang, the visit to the USSR affirmed two things. First, the reinvention of Chinee classical dance and introducing it through the art of Peking opera made Peking opera accessible to a world audience; dance became a world stage language. Second, as Peking opera's international position came to be recognized, maintaining its aesthetic performing system while introducing new aesthetic forms became a primary goal of Mei Lanfang. The dynamic rela-tionship between realism and symbolism was captured in the photo with which I opened the paper.

The visit and the exchanges that took place helped both sides to move for-ward with renewed insights into the artistic dilemmas that they faced at the time. Cultural interaction is necessarily asymmetrical. In this case, the Chinese theater, as I pointed out above, was struggling to be relevant in the coming of the mod-

ern world. Theater reform was called upon by Chinese theater reformers. As Mei
Lanfang and the Peking opera were seeking the path forward, Western realism
was the standard to which Chinese theater was attempting to conform. The visit
to America in 1930 and the visit to the USSR convinced Mei Lanfang that "being traditional" – albeit in a highly modified form – was the path forward.

The study of Mei's performance program and the filming of the opera provides us with an x-ray of the process through which Peking opera was integrated
into a global theater aesthetic. The process of this transcultural exchange was
captured by the filming of "Rainbow Pass," where theater art merged with film.
This singular event demonstrates the dynamics of cultural exchange, where both
sides become open to new concepts and ideas as they readjust their presentations.
This readjustment in turn helps new ideas and forms find local expression, and in
the process generate creative insights into one's own work inspired by what was
once foreign and unknown.

Bibliography

Eisenstein, Sergei. 1935. "The Enchanter from the Pear Garden: Introducing
     to Russian Audiences a Visitor from China." *Theater Arts Monthly* 19 (10):
     766–76, 770.
———. 1935. Film. Mei Lanfang performing section of "Rainbow Pass." On-
     line weblink: https://www.youtube.com/watch?v=4nlf5LW_nrQ.
Goldstein, Joshua. 2007. *Drama Kings: Players and Publics in the Recreation of
     Peking Opera, 1870–1937.* Berkeley.
Jiang, Ji. 2022. "Dongfang gudian xiju 'xianshizhuyi' wenti de 'shen xin' zhi
     huan yu zai yujinghua – yi gewu ji, jingju fang Su gongyan wei zhongxin"
     [The "Body versus Mind" Discussion Relating to "realism" in East Asia
     Classical Theater Re-contextualized through Performances of Kabuki and
     Peking Opera in the Soviet Union]. *Wenyi Yinjiu* 4, online publication:
     https://www.fx361.com/page/2022/0613/10717230.shtml.
Mei Lanfang. 1962. *Wo de dianying shenghuo* [My Film Career]. Beijing.
Mei Lanfang, and Anne Rebull. 2010. "Befriending Eisenstein on My First Trip
     to the Soviet Union." *The Opera Quarterly* 26 (2–3): 426–34.
Mei Shaowu, ed. 1997. *Mei Lanfang (daxing hua zhuan)* [A large-format picto-
     rial biography of Mei Lanfang]. Beijing.
*Performances of Mei Lan-Fang in Soviet Russia – Synopses of Plays and Dances
     Selected from His Repertoire.* 1935. Privately published.
Saussy, Haun. 2006. "Mei Lanfang. In Moscow, 1935: Familiar, Unfamiliar,
     Defamiliar." *Modern Chinese Literature and Culture* 18 (1): 8–29.
Scott, A. C. 1959. *Mei Lanfang, Leader of the Pear Garden.* Hong Kong.

Tian, Min. 2012. *Mei Lanfang and the Twentieth-Century International Stage Chinese Theatre Placed and Displaced.* New York.

Yeh, Catherine. 2016. "Experimenting with Dance Drama: Peking Opera Modernity, Kabuki Theater Reform and the Denishawn's Tour of the Far East." *Journal of Global Theatre History* 1 (2): 28–37.

———. 2020. "Mei Lanfang and Modern Dance: Transcultural Innovation in Peking Opera, 1910s–1920s." In *Corporeal Politics: Dancing East Asia,* edited by Katherine Mezur and Emily Wilcox. Ann Arbor, MI.

———. 2007. "Refined Beauty, New Woman, Dynamic Heroine or Fighter for the Nation?: Perceptions of China in the Programme Selection for Mei Lanfang's Performances in Japan (1919), the United States (1930), and the Soviet Union." *European Journal of East Asian Studies* 6 (1): 75–102.

Contributors

Manuela Coppola is affiliated faculty at Emerson College and holds a PhD in cultural and postcolonial studies from the Università di Napoli "L'Orientale." She is the author of two books and several journal articles on contemporary Caribbean poetry, feminist translation, resistance literature, and postcolonial Italian writing, and is the co-editor of a volume on gender and translation studies. She is currently working on two book projects on whiteness and the transcultural circulation of knowledge in Caribbean plantation society, and on the Malay ethnobotanical sources of Emilio Salgari's Italian novels.

Elizabeth C. Goldsmith is professor emerita of French at Boston University. Her publications have focused on cultural practices that influenced the literature of the early modern period: conversation, letter-writing, and memoirs. Her books include *Exclusive Conversations: The Art of Interaction in Seventeenth-Century French Literature* (1988), *Publishing Women's Life Stories in France, 1642–1720: From Voice to Print* (2001), and *The Kings' Mistresses: The Liberated Lives of Marie Mancini, Princess Colonna and Her Sister Hortense, Duchess Mazarin* (2012). She has edited and co-edited several collections of essays on epistolary literature and the history of women's writing in France. Her current research has been focusing on early travel narratives.

Eugenio Menegon received his training in Chinese language and culture at the Ca' Foscari University of Venice in Italy and earned an MA in Asian studies and PhD in history from the University of California at Berkeley. He teaches Chinese and world history in the Department of History at Boston University and is the author of many publications on Chinese-European exchanges and missionary history. His current book project is an examination of the daily life and political networking of European residents at the Qing court in Beijing during the 17th–18th centuries.

Roberta Micallef is professor of the practice in world languages and literatures and women, gender, and sexuality studies at Boston University. She received her PhD in comparative literature in 1997 from the University of Texas in Austin. In addition to being an avid traveler, Micallef has a longstanding interest in travel literature. She is the co-editor of *On the Wonders of Land and Sea: Persianate Travel Writing* (2013) and editor of *Illusion and Disillusionment: Travel Writing in the Modern Age* (2018). Both volumes were the outcomes of meetings by the faculty research group on travel literature. Micallef is also interested in Turkish literature, cultural products, and Turkish language instruction. She has contributed articles on these topics to edited volumes and journals over the years.

Mary Beth Raycraft received her PhD in French literature from NYU and has held faculty positions at Boston University and Vanderbilt University. Her research focuses on 19th- and 20th-century French women travelers. Her translation of Madame Léon Grandin's 1895 book, *Une Parisienne à Chicago* was published by the University of Illinois Press (2010). In addition to articles in *The French Review, Forum for Modern Language Studies,* and *Women in French Studies,* she is a co-author of the French textbook *Affaires globales,* published by Georgetown University Press (2021).

Sunil Sharma is professor of Persianate and comparative literature at Boston University's Department of Languages and Literatures and director of the Global Medieval Studies program. He is the author of several books on various aspects of medieval and early modern Persianate literary cultures and has translated poetry and travel writing from Persian and Urdu. His most recent book was *Three Centuries of Travel Writing by Muslim Women* (co-edited by Siobhan Lambert-Hurley and Daniel Majchrowicz; Indiana University Press, 2022). With another contributor to this volume, Robert Micallef, he co-edited a collection of essays, *On the Wonders of Land and Sea: Persianate Travel Writing* (Ilex, 2011).

James Uden is professor and department chair of classical studies at Boston University. He is the author of *The Invisible Satirist: Juvenal and Second-Century Rome* (2015) and *Spectres of Antiquity: Classical Literature and the Gothic, 1740-1830* (2020), and editor of *Worlds of Knowledge in Women's Travel Writing* (2022). He is currently writing books on Latin epic and ancient medicine.

Catherine V. Yeh is professor of Chinese literature and transcultural studies at Boston University. Her research interest is in global cultural interaction and flow in the fields of literature, media, and visual culture during the nineteenth and twentieth centuries. Her most recent books and projects include *The Chinese Political Novel: Migration of a World Genre* (Harvard University Press, 2015) and *Asia at the World's Fairs: An Online Exhibition of Cultural Exchange* (Project editor and co-author, Boston University 2018). Her current project is *Improbable Stars: Female Impersonators, Peking Opera and the Birth of Modern Star Culture in 1910s China.*